THE MODERN LAWYER
MARKETING STRATEGIES, TIPS & TOOLS

"Marketing is less daunting after reading this book which provides invaluable tips for simple strategies that I can implement in my practice, without a large budget. The content marketing suggestions are invaluable, easy to implement and are not costly. I would recommend that this book should be read by sole practitioners, and junior lawyers would also benefit from it. The book resonated with me more than other marketing courses or information that I have been given, because Mira clearly understands the mindset of lawyers and the culture of law firms. I have no doubt that I will revisit this book for marketing guidance as my business continues."

>**Fiona McCord**
>*Base Legal*

"Mira provides straightfoward, practical and easy to follow advice on how to become a progressive and innovative lawyer in the modern digital age. By following her tips and by understanding Mira's marketing methodologies, any lawyer will be able to propel both their career and legal practice forward to achieve ultimate success. A great read from an inspiring lawyer, entrepreneur, and very successful business owner. 5 stars!"

>**Karen Finch**
>*Family Lawyer*

"Mira was always responsive and answered all our questions. Mira has many years of experience in the legal profession. She is knowledgeable, always professional and acts with integrity and honesty."

>**Teresa Lamanna**
>*Better Health Nutrition*

THE MODERN LAWYER
MARKETING STRATEGIES, TIPS & TOOLS

MIRA STAMMERS

Australian Scholarly

Published 2018 by
Australian Scholarly Publishing Pty Ltd
7 Lt Lothian St Nth, North Melbourne, Vic 3051

Tel: 03 9329 6963 / Fax: 03 9329 5452
enquiry@scholarly.info / www.scholarly.info

ISBN 978-1-925588-66-8

Cover design: Amelia Walker
Photographer: Nancy Morrison
Stylist: Peta-Gai McLaughlin, Iridis Cosmetics

To Lachlan, for making me strive every day to be the best mum I can be. I am truly blessed to have you in my life.

Contents

Chapter 3

Chapter 4

Introduction

Welcome to *The Modern Lawyer*. You've made a great decision to invest in this book.

Being a lawyer can come with a lot of ups and downs, particularly in today's market. The competition is fierce and the market is changing. We need all the support we can get. So let me share my journey with you; let me tell you about how I came to write this book, and why I think it will help you get the commercial advantage you've been looking for.

For me, one of my biggest career challenges was making the decision to leave my role as a Senior Associate in London and move back home to Melbourne. You see, I had been told that I was about to be put on the fast track to partnership and, while that sounded fantastic, it also meant living permanently in London. I decided I wanted to be close to family, so after a bit of travel I moved home.

When I arrived back in Melbourne, I started to look for work as a banking lawyer, but I became frustrated when I saw what was happening to the legal profession in Australia. So many lawyers seemed dissatisfied with the inflexible nature of the work, so they either left the profession entirely (particularly women) or left the big firms to start their own practices.

Clients also seemed dissatisfied on a number of levels, but particularly with lawyers that charged for every phone call and every email. Clients constantly felt anxious about fees and the lack of price certainty.

I wanted to change this. I wanted lawyers to be able to work flexibly, and I wanted clients to have access to lawyers who worked on a fixed-fee pricing structure. So I went about launching Legally Yours (legallyyours.com.au), a legal marketplace where clients could access fixed-fee lawyers around Australia who work from their home or office via the phone or internet. This gave clients the satisfaction of price certainty, and lawyers the ability to work virtually and flexibly.

I managed to get sixty lawyers around Australia on board and had a big launch party. I felt ready for an exciting new adventure, but unfortunately it was very slow to take off. A few family and friends used the service, and referrals were starting to happen, but that wasn't enough to sustain the business. You see, while I had a business plan, I hadn't yet learnt how to market the business effectively. So I started to learn, and learn, and learn. I engaged coaches, read books and completed courses. I was determined to make Legally Yours a success. The hard work paid off because Legally Yours hit six figures in revenue in its first year, has consistently grown since launch and has attracted investors.

Launching and running a legal marketplace that operates under the 'new law' paradigm taught me a lot. It also attracted a lot of attention and a lot of questions from lawyers about how they can grow and adapt their practice. Though I already teach and consult on these matters, I wanted to reach more people. That was the start of this journey to write a book and share my strategies with you.

In this book, you will learn about a variety of different marketing strategies, tips and tools. Some will appeal to you more than others, so this book is designed to give you a snapshot of different strategies so you can decide which ones are right for you.

We will start by challenging your mindset around marketing so that you're in the right frame of mind before you implement any of the tips and tools. We will move on to how you can step inside your client's mind and discover what they really need from you (and thus how to market to them). We will explore strategies to attract new clients to your practice, and will also discuss how you can make more profit from the clients you already have. Finally, I'll leave you with some tips and tools for planning your future.

The book is best read in a linear fashion (and, knowing lawyers, I'm sure you will do this!) but if you want to chop and change, you can do that, provided you have first read Chapters 1 and 2.

I hope you use this book to create the practice you desire. To your success!

Chapter 1

Making Your Mark

"Making your mark on the world is hard. If it were easy, everybody would do it. But it's not. It takes patience, it takes commitment, and it comes with plenty of failure along the way. The real test is not whether you avoid this failure, because you won't. It's whether you let it harden or shame you into inaction, or whether you learn from it; whether you choose to persevere."

Barack Obama

Making your mark as a lawyer starts with making a name for yourself within the profession, and ideally ends with making a positive and meaningful contribution to the profession as a whole. To accomplish these goals, you first need to be known for what you do, and that starts with marketing.

Why is marketing your law firm so important?

As with any business, a law firm cannot survive or flourish without a solid base of clients. While many lawyers are aware of the importance of marketing, most don't give it priority. Even if it makes it onto the 'to do' list, it's generally right down the bottom.

For sole practitioners, this is usually because they don't know how to effectively market themselves (so they put it off), or otherwise they don't believe they have the time to focus on marketing.

For junior lawyers, often the exposure to marketing opportunities is limited because the partners don't want to expose juniors to important clients. This results in lawyers having almost no experience in marketing by the time they make partner, but by then it's too late as the pressure to bring in clients is already in full swing. Even if you're at a firm that is exposing you to marketing opportunities as a junior practitioner, you're rarely given any training or support to help you turn those opportunities into profits.

Whatever your reason for not marketing yourself consistently and effectively, it's time for those reasons to disappear. Taking the time to learn to market yourself, either in your own practice or as part of your skill set as a junior practitioner, is vital to your success.

Ultimately, the success of one's practice is twofold. Not only must you have the requisite experience to advise your clients, but you must also be able to identify your client's problems, and communicate to them why you're best placed to be able to help them solve their problems.

The difficulty that many lawyers face is that while they know how to 'network', they simply don't know how to effectively market their skill set. So many lawyers are incredibly talented, but what they lack is an ability to communicate their offering to the market and stand out from the crowd.

It's important to know your skill set well so that you can be clear about where you sit in the marketplace. Once you understand what you have to offer, you can target the right client base for your practice, making it easy for clients to say 'yes' to your services. Demonstrating thought leadership, becoming an expert in your field and raising your profile will also serve you well. As with any business, knowing your client base intimately, staying relevant and solving your client's problems are key. After all, no one wants to become the next Kodak of the legal world.

Marketing does not need to be daunting, overwhelming, expensive or time-consuming. You can in fact enjoy being creative and innovative in your thinking once you understand what the market really wants. Just spending some time each week focusing on marketing your business will not only help you increase your profits, but you might even have a bit of fun in the process!

There are incredible opportunities to market your firm's services and to show your clients that you can solve their problems. This book will help you explore those opportunities and hopefully make marketing an enjoyable part of your practice.

Why 'selling' is not a dirty word

While many lawyers will eventually get comfortable with the idea that they need to 'market' their services, in my experience few are comfortable with 'selling' their services. Let me explain by way of an example. Many lawyers are happy to identify prospects and communicate their capabilities to those prospects, but they don't try to qualify the prospects, handle objections, actively seek to close the sale or follow-up on lost prospects when not hired.

When I ask lawyers why this seems to be the case I often get the following responses:

'It's unprofessional to overtly sell your services.'

'I don't want to pressure people.'

'I'm not in sales, I'm a professional with many years of experience. People will use my services simply because I'm good at what I do.'

Or the most common one: 'Overtly 'selling' legal services violates our traditions, ethics and our status in society. I don't want to be seen as an ambulance chaser. I'd rather just focus on doing legal work.'

My response to these objections is that, if you're engaged in running a law firm as a business, you need to be engaged in selling.

It's important to get clear that if you're a legal practitioner, particularly if you're a sole practitioner, you must learn to sell. End of story.

Being great at what you do is of course crucial, but it's only a baseline measurement for your success. There are a lot of technically brilliant practitioners out there, but many of them don't have a thriving practice. If they are working within a firm, they often don't get promoted. Instead, they end up doing the grunt work for a partner of the firm who is able to sell.

Selling is not just about presenting all the information to clients, then letting them decide whether they feel it's appropriate to buy what you're offering. It's also not enough to rely on the fact that your services are so exceptional they should sell themselves. It is your job to make the sale – to close the sale.

Once you're clear about what your job is, you no longer have mixed agendas. Mixed agendas often get in the way of making a sale. An example of a mixed agenda might be a need to be liked or accepted, or a fear of doing things that may put pressure on a client to buy from you.

As a lawyer, you're in the game of selling your services. The great thing is that you get to choose exactly how you get to do that. You don't have to ever do it in a way that compromises your professional standards, and nor should you.

Now that we're clear that 'selling' your services is essential to any business that relies on revenue to survive, let's have a look at exactly what you need to get started.

Why your beliefs could be holding you back

Over the years I've had some very in-depth, honest conversations with lawyers. Some of these lawyers have been practising for years and are equity partners in big international firms. Even amongst these elite, successful, credible lawyers, there remained some self-doubt. It's not that surprising. After all, being a lawyer can be tough. There's no room for error, and it's highly competitive field.

This self-doubt might be consistently present, or it might flow in and out of your work life, depending on how things are tracking. What does seem to be consistent is that most lawyers at some point in time get plagued by a feeling that perhaps they don't really know what they're doing or that one day they'll be 'found out'. This is true of even the most technically talented lawyers I know. Perhaps it is indicative of being in a field where mistakes are 'not allowed to happen'.

Whatever the cause, these negative thoughts you may be having create fear, fear that holds you back from the very opportunities that lie directly in front of you. A lot of lawyers I've spoken to fear judgment; in other words, they fear that they aren't as confident or talented as other lawyers around them. After all, there does seem to be a lot of bravado in the profession.

Let's be really clear about this. You're not only holding yourself back, but you're making a lot of assumptions about other people that are probably incorrect. If you think about it for a moment, the same beliefs that you have, most other people have too. Those very people you believe might be smarter than you, more confident than you, or more successful than you, may actually be feeling exactly the same way you feel.

The first step you need to take in order to move forward is to acknowledge your internal dialogue and realise how negative it is. The next step is to challenge those negative self-thoughts. What evidence do you have for thinking this way? Is thinking this way serving you in any way? Do you believe this to be true? Just by using these simple steps, you'll understand that perhaps some of these beliefs are based on false assumptions that don't really stand up when scrutinised.

To challenge these thoughts, try writing down some positive beliefs or thoughts about yourself. List your achievements, perhaps some clients you've won, people you've helped in your career, the difference you've made for people.

When you catch yourself having negative self-thoughts, it's important to replace them with positive thoughts as best you can. Remind yourself what you have to offer. Everyone has something to offer.

Have a think about what you truly want to achieve, and work backwards. Be clear about your goals, be clear about your vision, be clear about your core beliefs and the 'why', then let go of the safety net and just go for it. Forget perfectionism; it's holding you back.

Why the world has changed, and so must you

My true belief is that over the next few years, law firms will need to undergo dramatic change in the way that they market their services and use technology. They will either transform themselves into relevant marketable services, or they will simply be left behind.

The current global legal marketplace is certainly digital; there's no denying it. New business models are being developed every day and law is certainly a profession where new business models are starting to disrupt the way things have always been. Think about it: the traditional 'lawyer' route is to get a degree or two in law, get a job at a law firm (or open your own eventually), increase your expertise and perhaps specialise, and *then* learn to market your skill set to attract clients. If you're doing well, you might employ staff members who follow in your footsteps.

The cycle goes on. The same traditional marketing methods are utilised and lawyers continue to practise law with little regard for the fact that they are actually running a business that's all about *outcomes* for clients.

There are of course exceptions to the rule, but in general I have found lawyers to be appalling managers. In many law firms, management is simply lacking or doesn't exist. Leadership is nowhere to be found, there's no long-term strategic plan, no marketing goals, strategy or vision, and generally no sense of direction. The best most firms come up with is a set of core values. Whether or not they follow them is another question.

So why am I starting this book in such a negative way? Because I fundamentally believe law firms need to flip this on its head. They need to implement change and they need to run their businesses as businesses, either by developing the appropriate management and marketing skills themselves, or by utilising experts in those areas to assist them. It is only when we start to view law firms as actual businesses focused on closing sales and hitting revenue targets that we are able to make some progress and discover innovative, progressive ways to stand out from the crowd in the current competitive marketplace.

In fact, law seems to be one of the few professions where there's still incredible opportunity to stand out – if only we let go of the reluctance to explore new ways of delivering legal services.

The choice is yours. Be a progressive thought leader and control the future of your firm or be a victim of the impending change. By investing in this book, it seems you've made a great choice to be part of a legal revolution, and I couldn't be happier.

By using the tips in this book you'll start to develop a business and marketing mindset where you're focusing on the key things that will actually help you grow and stand out from the crowd.

How much time do you need to get started?

Running a law firm can be a busy process. It takes a lot of effort to get it up and running, and a lot of effort to keep it going. It's important, however, to consider how much time you're working 'in the business' as opposed to 'on the business'.

Marketing is certainly an activity where you focus on working 'on the business' to grow it in order to increase revenue. Now while most lawyers obviously understand this concept, it doesn't mean that much changes. Lawyers continue to do the work that comes in and only pop their head up to see what's going on when things start to slow down. Even if marketing efforts are employed, they're often not consistent.

Marketing can certainly feel overwhelming. Many lawyers worry it will take them away from doing their 'real work' which makes them money. Add to that the fact that it can be very hard to decide where to start and you've got yourself in a position of procrastination.

Of course, you can spend a lot of time and money on legal marketing, but it's not necessary.

You also don't have to be a rainmaker to help your business improve. What is necessary, however, is to have a clearly focused marketing strategy, one that concentrates on the activities that you do well and the activities that you enjoy.

This book outlines a vast array of marketing activities that can be undertaken, but the key here is to select those that fit your ideal customer as well as those which suit where you sit in the marketplace. If you have a clearly defined marketing plan that focuses on the right audience and you carry out these activities on a consistent basis, you needn't dedicate that much time at all, because each activity and part of the plan will be focused on generating maximum outcomes for minimum inputs.

In determining exactly how much time you need to spend on

marketing each day or each week, remember to be reasonable and realistic about your goals. Setting large goals may result in failure, so I would suggest starting with a small goal, perhaps on a weekly basis.

Perhaps the goal might be to deliver one valuable blog to your client base per week. You could then allocate fifteen minutes or half an hour per day to draft this blog so that by the end of the week you've actually spend two and a half hours on marketing and you've delivered some valuable content to your readers.

Alternatively perhaps your focus is on social media, which in some ways can be even easier. For this goal you might set a target of tweeting once or twice a day, or sharing a piece of content on Facebook on a daily basis.

Whatever the goal, as long as it's realistic, achievable and measureable, you're on your way.

How much money do you need to get started?

A common question I hear in relation to legal marketing is, 'How much money do I need to spend to get results?' The reality is, I don't necessarily believe that the more you spend, the better the outcome. Some firms spend a large amount of money on PR, but they may not actually be getting the results they want for their money.

Initially, it will be about testing different marketing channels to see what works for you. Once you understand that a particular marketing channel delivers return on investment, that's the marketing channel to focus on and put money into.

What I can guarantee you is that marketing your firm does not necessarily require a large initial outlay of capital. There are many ideas included in this book that are free and simply require time. If time is not something you feel you have much of, of course feel free to outsource tasks and pay for them. There are many outsourcing platforms these days that provide third party marketers for your business at low cost (try fiverr.com or airtasker.com).

The important thing to remember is that, whenever you're spending money on marketing, you need to measure each marketing channel you're using so you can determine whether or not you're getting the results you hoped for.

What you will need to avoid is wasting money on marketing strategies that aren't measurable or aren't delivering results. A lot of people make this mistake with radio advertising. They believe if they get their brand name out there to such a large audience, they'll get a lot of new clients. But they fail to consider their target market when making this choice and therefore often end up wasting a lot of money. In addition, it's very hard to measure the success of radio advertising unless you're offering something specifically for that group of clients, or unless you're providing a separate phone number so you can record the number of phone calls that come in from that campaign.

Alternatively, writing a blog and posting it on LinkedIn costs you no money, uses a small amount of your time, and you're able to gauge quite easily how many people read and engage with your blog. This allows you to measure how valuable that content is to your audience. In fact these days you can also track how many visitors you've had to your website based on that blog.

The key here is that you don't need a lot of money to get started – in fact you need none – but you do need to have channels that are measurable so that when you start spending some money, you're using the right channels to do so. Once you have found those channels, it's important that you consider how much growth you require in your business and how fast you want to achieve that growth.

For instance, a very aggressive marketer would ensure that all profits in the business after paying wages, either to yourself or to your staff, are put back into the company for further growth and development of marketing channels. Other law firms that are less aggressive in the marketing department might allocate a percentage of their revenue per annum on marketing and are happy with that.

As long as you can measure the return on investment and as long as you're getting $1.05 back for every $1 that you spend, your marketing budget is actually unlimited.

How to get results by using this book

This book is intended for the busy practitioner. It is not a book that you have to read in an orderly fashion from start to end; it's a book that you can simply pick up and focus on one chapter or one tip to get you started. It is a book that allows you to learn something new in just ten minutes a day, should you wish to set that time aside.

The best way to get results fast by using this book is to read the next chapter in full and focus on understanding and implementing one tip per week from the remaining chapters. Not all tips will be right for you or right for your practice, but that's okay. Just choose the tips that resonate with you. Perhaps start with some easy ones first and consistently implement them each week.

If you get lost at any stage, it's important to reflect back on chapters one and two so that you really understand why you're doing what you're doing and what you have to offer the marketplace. These two chapters form a foundation for implementing the rest of the tips in the book.

I look forward to helping you achieve your business goals.

Chapter 2

Who Are You and What Do You Want?

"The secret of change is to focus all of your energy not on fighting the old, but on building the new."

Socrates

Before you're able to come up with a strategic plan, or a marketing plan for that matter, it's very important to be clear about two things. First, you need to know exactly who you are and what you do. Second, you need to know who you want to help and why (i.e. what problem are you trying to solve?). This might sound obvious, but it's incredible how few lawyers have spent time delving into these matters in depth.

When you're clear about what you have to offer and what problem you're trying to solve, you can focus on an appropriate message to send to your target market to encourage them to engage you.

This chapter looks at how you can differentiate yourself in the market by emphasising your true competitive differences. After all, who wants to be 'just another lawyer' who's hoping for 'just another client'?

Creating a niche

The first step in making your business stand out from the crowd is to develop a business niche. Law is a highly competitive field. Whether you provide services to businesses or consumers, there are hundreds of lawyers out there who do exactly what you do. Without a niche, you're likely to fade into the background. This is true whether you own your own firm or work within a firm. You need to be known for what you're good at.

If you develop a niche and become known for what you specialise in, you'll find clients start coming to you because your expertise is demonstrated within the market, ultimately making you and your services more valuable.

Niches can be used in a range of ways, though most lawyers tend to find a niche in a particular area of law. It's much easier to build your profile and accordingly build a financially successful practice if you focus on one area of law and become quite specialised in that area. Once you find your niche, you'll be able to do the following:

- command high pricing
- receive referrals from other lawyers, because they don't view you as a competitor
- understand the problems facing your client group (and fix them).

I've had many lawyers tell me that once they've found a niche for their practice, they've doubled, even quadrupled, their revenue.

Sometimes having a 'double niche' can also be extremely effective. Imagine for a moment that you're a commercial lawyer and your niche is in business law, but you have a double niche where you work solely with business coaches. At networking events you talk to people about your specialty in working with business coaches. It's memorable. People understand it, and they quickly understand what you do, without effort. The next time they speak with a business coach who has a legal issue, guess who's coming to mind? You!

Ensuring your niche is profitable

One of the main benefits of finding a niche for your practice is to be able to understand your target market well. Once you understand your market, you can understand the legal problems they face on quite a deep level. Then you fix those problems and promote yourself as the expert in solving those particular problems.

However, keep in mind that the niche you choose is very important, because if you choose a niche that's not profitable or that doesn't have an attractive proposition to the market, your revenue figures could actually go down. The goal here is to choose a niche in a particular area of law which reflects your experience and one in which you enjoy working.

You also have the option to further divide that niche into a smaller niche, perhaps one with smaller market segments that have specific interests and demographics.

For instance, the market for business lawyers is quite large, so you may wish to focus on one or two types of professionals whom you'll aim to help on a regular basis. For example, you might like to work with vets or digital marketers or franchisors. The trick here is to choose a niche that not only has enough demand but also is quite profitable.

One doesn't necessarily follow the other. Take personal trainers as an example. They may need legal protection within their business more than most, but they may not have the budget for it or wish to spend their money on legal services; hence, the demand is not there to warrant a niche in that area.

To ensure your niche is profitable, there are a number of steps to follow as outlined in this chapter, including understanding your ideal client, understanding the core problem that you're solving for that client and making sure that your ideal customer is actually willing to pay to resolve that problem. Let's take a look at these in more detail.

Understanding your ideal client

Now you've chosen your niche, it's time to understand exactly who your ideal client is. If you don't understand your ideal client well, you'll likely miss the mark when you try to market your services to them. If you do understand your ideal client well, you'll save yourself a lot of time and a lot of money.

Take the time to ask yourself the following questions about the demographic features of your ideal client:

- how old are they?
- what gender are they?
- where do they live?
- how much do they earn?
- how often do they use legal services?

Once you've asked yourself these questions, you should also research how big this particular market is. For instance, if your ideal client is a male business owner in the eastern suburbs with one to ten employees and an annual revenue of $5,000,000, the market for your ideal client might be quite small. You'd need to review your parameters and expand them to identify a larger target market.

Once you've set your parameters and understand the demographics of your ideal client, it's time to understand what legal problems they are facing and how you might help them solve those problems.

Let's take, as an example, a business lawyer who has chosen to work with male business coaches aged between twenty-five and forty-five, earning at least $100,000 in Melbourne. That lawyer must understand the legal problems that those business coaches have. They may need help with their business structure, they may be having challenges with their terms and conditions or they're looking to grow by acquiring another business.

It's important here not to waste time and money guessing what products and services your prospective clients may need. Ask them. Ask many of them. Once you understand their problems and their needs, create a solution specifically for them, and promote that solution to them.

By having a better understanding of your ideal client, you can target that specific client group and ask them what problems they face and how you might be able to help. That way, you can create solutions that are tailored to them. Basically, you find out the problem, and fix it. If you can do that, you are automatically creating value for your clients and your clients will pay for your services.

Here are some questions to ask your target market:

- what frustrates them in relation to legal services?
- what do they lose sleep over at night?
- what are their biggest objections to doing business with you?
- where do they network and gather?
- who have they used as lawyers before you?
- most importantly, what do they want and/or need when it comes to legal services?

For the most part, lawyers commonly think they know this information, so they fail to ask questions of their target market. They base their legal solutions on anecdotal evidence and often miss the mark completely. This is wonderful news for you as they are your competition.

Remember that market research is not just a one-time thing. If you want to stay current, relevant and progressive in your market, you need to regularly update your market intelligence.

What is the core problem you're solving?

As outlined above, regardless of the niche you have chosen, if you don't take the time to understand your ideal client and help them solve a problem, you probably won't be all that profitable. The problem also has to be big enough to warrant spending money fixing it. So ask yourself, have you done enough research into your ideal client group to understand in depth what core problem you're solving? If not, keep researching. Every minute spent on understanding the problem will save you hours in the future with your marketing efforts.

If you're still not quite clear, start spending time where your ideal client spends time. Talk to them, ask them questions, listen to the answers and ask more questions. Look at online groups where your ideal clients have discussions, have a look at their websites, get out there and network with them. It should start to become clear.

This type of work is what I see lawyers failing to do everyday. If they do this work at all, they do it after the fact, almost unintentionally when they're networking with their current client base. The intention here is to plan for the kind of clients you want to work with.

When I started Legally Yours, I went out to every single business owner I knew and asked them to tell me everything that they hated about lawyers – everything. I listened for hours about their complaints. Every complaint helped me understand how the legal profession had failed them. This was a huge opportunity as it made me get really clear on how I could do something different to help them. These complaints formed the basis for my plan to solve their problems by delivering exactly the opposite of what they had previously encountered.

Once you've found your niche market and understand the biggest problems that face that market, you've basically done more work than most, and you've drastically improved your chances of success. All you need to do now is find a solution to at least one of their major problems.

Is your ideal client willing to pay to resolve the problem?

So you have a target market now (your niche), and you have a clear understanding of what problems that market faces. You've had a think about what services you can offer to solve your target market's biggest problems. That's great. Now ask yourself, is the service that you're offering a 'must have' or a 'nice to have' service? The more your service is a 'must have' service, the more profitable you will be.

As you know, prospective clients are overwhelmed with choice on a daily basis. Attention spans are getting shorter and very few service providers are being noticed. So you need to be solving real and painful problems for your niche. The more painful the problem, the more your solution becomes a 'must have' solution.

What are the biggest legal problems your target market is facing? Do they know they have this problem or do you need to educate them? Can you solve their problems in a smarter or faster way than other service providers? Clients who are aware of their legal problems and who are motivated to address them are very easy to market to, as you don't need to educate them or convince them of the value of your services. They already need you.

Creating a 'must have' service is also a lot about value creation. You need to create a service that demonstrates so much value for your prospective client base that it becomes a 'no-brainer' decision. Value creation can be achieved in a number of ways. Sometimes the value is in the accessibility to you or to information you have. Other times the value might be in how you offer flexible payment terms (i.e. payment plans that make the fees seem more manageable). By creating more value, you're automatically reducing the likelihood of objections from clients about why they should use your service.

It's important to test and validate your idea. The more you test your theory, the more likely it will be that you identify a market that has a problem they are willing to pay to solve. After all, if your target market isn't willing to pay you to solve their legal problems, you don't really have a business, you have a hobby.

Keep asking questions

Markets change, clients change, problems change. To stay relevant, you need to keep asking questions and adapting your offers to what your clients need at any given time.

You'll need to stay on top of who your ideal client is, always. Never think that this information is stagnant and that who your ideal client was two years ago is still who they are today.

Once you have built a client base of your 'target market', it's much easier to update this information on a regular basis as they are right in front of you. Stay connected with what their attitudes are, what interests they have, how they live their life and what challenges and frustrations they have. You may gain a lot of this information by holding regular networking evenings, by taking them out to lunch or perhaps by visiting their workplace. It doesn't matter *how* you accomplish this goal, as long as you stay connected. The more connected you are to your target market, the more relevant you are.

Continue to get out of your comfort zone and speak with prospective clients. Talk to them about your ideas and your services. Ask them how you might best help them. How could you make their life easier? What drives them when making purchasing decisions? Are they currently using legal services? Who are they using? Why have they been with them for so long?

A lot of prospective clients have stayed with the same lawyer simply because they haven't taken the time to find another one. Often they even have a multitude of complaints about their current lawyer. That makes your job a lot easier because you can show them the value of your service offering and how you're different from the lawyer they're currently using.

Many lawyers become complacent with their client base, thinking that it's all about loyalty and that clients won't change lawyers. But don't forget, clients are getting savvier and more demanding. They want someone who is focused on them and their needs. So the more questions you ask, the more relevant you will become and the more opportunities you will have. Don't be afraid to continue to ask questions.

Deciding how to deliver your services

Deciding how to deliver your services comes down to what your target market expects in relation to delivery of services. How easy is it for them to engage your services? For instance, you might work from an office in the country, but you're not going to get many clients who are willing to drive out to see you. Perhaps then, you could work virtually to make your services more accessible.

Some other questions you may ask include:

- what are their expectations in relation to service delivery?
- do they expect access to you outside of business hours?
- do they want all forms of communication, including Skype and virtual consultations?
- do they care whether you have big, fancy offices?

This last question is important as it can affect your bottom line dramatically. If your target market doesn't necessarily expect face-to-face communication or fancy offices, your overheads can be reduced dramatically by working virtually.

When launching Legally Yours, I asked clients whether they were happy to instruct their lawyers virtually or whether they'd prefer to go into physical offices to speak with their lawyers. To my surprise, nine out of ten people I asked said they were very happy to instruct lawyers virtually, particularly if there were options for out of hours appointments.

Phone consultations, Skype consultations and the like are now in demand. It makes sense. People are busy these days and can't necessarily take time out of their work day to visit their lawyer's office. For Legally Yours, delivering services virtually means that we can have lawyers in all different locations working virtually and flexibly, which is not only great for our target market, but also great for our lawyers.

It's important to ask your target market what their expectations are, and to meet those expectations. Whether you have a physical office or use technology to interact with your client base, try to make a decision about how you will operate your practice, and stick to it.

Fixed fee versus time-based billing

This subject is one that I'm very passionate about. It is also one that I've researched extensively for my own business. It is my belief that in this market and this economic climate, there's a lot of pressure on service providers to provide price certainty and value to their clients.

From my own experience when talking with clients, one of the biggest obstacles to engaging a lawyer is the existence of the dreaded hourly rate. Often lawyers will quote a large hourly rate and not be very clear about exactly how many hours it will take to achieve the outcome the client desires, leaving the client uncertain and anxious. Whilst the topic of fixed fee and value-based billing is the subject of another book, it's important to spend time considering whether you prefer to follow the billing methods that have traditionally been used, or whether you'd like to be a bit more progressive and innovative with the way you charge clients.

Again, this comes back to focusing on the client's needs, not your own. The billing method you use should reflect the requirements of your target market. In my experience, clients are screaming for fixed fees but lawyers are resisting this because of the unfounded belief that they will lose money. Alternatively, lawyers simply charge a fixed fee that reflects their hourly rate multiplied by how many hours they think the task will take to complete. This type of billing is, at its core, not creating any kind of value for the client, neither is it progressive nor innovative. There are books dedicated to this subject and seminars you can access if you want to find out more. I would urge you to at least consider these other options within your practice.

Fixed fee and value-based billing (these concepts can be quite different and come in many forms), can actually be as profitable, if not more profitable, than the hourly rate. This is particularly true if you learn to create products from your services and bundle those products to create maximum value to your client.

I also believe that fixed fees can be delivered on almost any project with the exception of some types of litigation. It's simply about being clear about the scope of work you will conduct, and being accountable to the client (i.e. revising the fee if the scope changes).

When I was working in London for a big international firm, we priced very large deals exceeding 400 million pounds on a fixed-fee basis. We understood that, to remain competitive, we needed to assume some risk. We mitigated this risk by understanding the matter in detail, scoping appropriately and revising the quote if the scope changed. My point here is that, if we were able to provide this kind of value to clients on large deals, the average lawyer in practice can certainly do the same for simple tasks like drafting a Shareholder's Agreement.

Whether you choose fixed fee, time-based billing or some combination of fixed fee and value-based billing, I'd encourage you to choose that specific billing method only after checking with your target market what works for them. I urge you to avoid charging hourly rates because that's what has always been done and because you don't want to have to learn new ways of operating. Don't forget, your choice about billing can be a competitive advantage in the marketplace. Not many people are being innovative in this space, so it's a chance to stand out from the crowd.

What is your 'why'?

Every day I watch business owners pitch their business to prospective clients. Every day they talk about their services or products. They describe the features of those services and products, and sometimes they discuss the pricing of those services and products. Sure, it makes sense, but it can certainly get a little boring. Who wants to hear a lawyer going on and on about the law and their experience? Even I don't want to hear that.

While what is being said is certainly very informative; people need connection. Sharing information about what you're offering is only part of what's needed. In and of itself, it will rarely close a sale. Talking about your experience is useful, but it's not what's going to connect you with the audience and close the sale. We've seen this too many times in the technology industry. Take smart phones or computers as examples. One brand of smartphone or computer may actually have better features and technology than its competitor, but its competitor doesn't solely focus on the features. That is, its competitor focuses not on the 'what' or the 'how', but the 'why'. They focus on value, on why they do what they do and why they're different, what they believe in, what they're passionate about. By changing their focus they connect with people on a different level, a personal level. It makes them memorable and makes their product important.

To demonstrate the point, think about prime ministers and presidents around the world, the ones who are most charismatic and remembered are the ones who talk about why they do what they do and why they believe in what they believe in. The 'why' never gets lost, whereas the 'what' and the 'how' often do.

Spend some time thinking about your 'why'. What is your passion? Why do you do what you do? What do you believe in? Then communicate those messages to your target market.

What are your core values?

Law firms often talk about their core values. Yet very few firms actually practice them, nor do they reflect on whether those values are still relevant to them today.

This topic is very much linked into your 'why'. Your core business values should reflect your vision for your business. If you reflect on your business now, what drives your behaviour in your business? What are the key foundations on which your business decisions sit?

There are a lot of benefits to clarifying your core values for your business. Primarily, when you are clear about your values, it becomes extremely easy to make business decisions because each decision is viewed in light of those values and must align with them. For instance, if one of your core values is transparency, and you're deciding on your pricing policy, you may wish to adopt a fixed-fee pricing model because it aligns nicely with one of your core values.

Not only do core values help you make better business decisions, they also help you educate your target market about what you stand for. In this sense, they can also be a useful resource for recruiting and retaining staff.

When you're deciding on core values, it's important to others (whether it's family, friends or clients), what they think your core values are. This helps you double-check whether you're on the right track and whether there's consistency between your beliefs and your actions in business.

Ideally, these core values shouldn't be related to money and they should hold steady, regardless of changes to the economic climate, because these core values will continue to be with your business, regardless of what happens over time. For instance, with my business, the core values were originally 'accessibility, affordability and transparency'. It was very important to me that people had access to legal advice, so we created a virtual business using technology that enabled multiple access points to lawyers at any time of the day or night. I also understood that a big barrier to accessing legal advice is a perception (whether true or not) that legal advice is unaffordable and therefore unattainable. Given this, I adopted a fixed-fee pricing policy to try to reduce anxiety around legal fees and give some price certainty to clients. Transparency was also important to me on a number of levels as I felt the legal profession was probably the least transparent profession in existence. Therefore, everything we do is based on transparency, from our pricing policy to the way we share information, to our communication and responsiveness. Even our business cards are transparent – literally.

Transparency has actually been one of my core drivers in terms of my business decisions. This core value informs the majority of my marketing decisions and helps me get clear on the partnership deals I am open to (and those I am not). I always ensure that I align myself with other companies that carry similar core values. If we don't share them, we don't work together. Here are some other examples of core values that might be relevant to you:

- accountability
- commitment
- diversity
- empowerment
- innovation
- integrity
- responsiveness
- safety
- balance
- encouragement.

So now you have your niche, with your ideal client, you understand the problem you're solving and that your customers are willing to pay for those problems to be solved. You're also clear about your billing method, you understand why you're doing what you're doing and what your core values are. Now let's look at your competition.

What's your competition?

Understanding your offering and the 'why' behind your offering are the most important foundational aspects of any business. The next most important aspect is being clear about who your competitors are, what they're offering and where they sit in the marketplace.

By having this information you'll be able to decide where you want to sit within the marketplace, how to price your services competitively and how to compete with the other firms that are already servicing your target market.

So, who are your competitors? Unless you're riding an incredibly new trend, you will have competitors. It might be quite clear to you who they are, or you might need to do some research. Even if you think you know whom your competitors are, I'd advise you to do some fact-checking because your competition is always changing.

You might gain this intelligence by doing internet searches, buying market reports or asking your target market who they're currently using. Once you've found who your main competitors are, have a look at the following:

- the range of products or services they provide
- how they market their products or services
- the prices they charge
- their distribution methods
- the referral or customer loyalty programs they implement
- their branding message
- whether they're innovative
- their culture and the size of their business
- whether they are leveraging technology and, if so, how
- who manages the business and what kind of person they are.

Once you have this information, you're going to know a lot more about your competitors, and thus a lot more about where you sit within the mix of legal service offerings. How do you compare to them?

My next recommendation is to actually get in contact with your competitors, ask them for a quote, have a consultation, experience their service. This will give you a much better understanding of the style of their business and the initial impressions they make on clients. Whatever you do, I'm a strong believer that competitors are friends, not enemies. You never know, you might be trying to solve exactly the same problem and perhaps you can learn from each other about how to solve it.

Obviously use your judgment with any information they volunteer or any advice they give. Ideally, you're looking to understand the following three things from the information you obtain:

- what you can learn from them / what you can do better
- what they're doing worse than you
- what they're doing the same as you.

If they're doing some things better than you, that's great! You can learn from them and innovate further, based on what seems to be working for them. If they seem to be good at giving value to their clients, how can you add more value? How can you exploit the gaps you've identified where perhaps they're not doing as well as you?

The more you can understand the competition and the more you stay innovative and relevant, the better you'll do.

Chapter 3
How To Attract New Clients

"The best way to find yourself is to lose yourself in the service of others."

Mahatma Gandhi

As a lawyer, you will be acutely aware that the success of your practice lies in your ability to attract and retain new clients. Increasing the number of clients you advise allows you to grow as a business owner and fulfil your career goals.

Now that you've spent time getting to know both what you have to offer the market and who your ideal client is, you're much better placed to target specific marketing channels to attract those ideal clients you seek.

That is, having a clear picture of your ideal client allows you to know where to start looking for those clients. Whom you seek to attract will differ for each and every practice; however, the concepts and strategies that can be applied will generally remain the same. This chapter outlines some proven marketing strategies for attracting new clients to your practice.

Understand your marketing channels

If you're currently working with clients, you've presumably got some marketing channels in place already, though perhaps you haven't clearly defined them for yourself just yet.

The marketing channels you should use for your practice will differ, depending on whether your ideal clients are businesses or consumers. In this sense, it's important to reflect on which marketing channels have already been working for you. If you're unclear of what has and has not worked for you in the past, it's time to get clear. Where are your clients coming from?

If you're not sure of the answer to this question, ask your clients how they found you. Once you start incorporating this question into your first conversation with new and prospective clients, you'll be better able to measure which marketing channels are already working effectively.

Most law firms I work with have historically attracted clients through very traditional marketing channels such as referrals, speaking opportunities and networking. Whichever methods you have been using, it's important to track their effectiveness so you know which channels to double down on and which channels to stop putting time and money into.

Keep those methods that are effective and broaden your horizons to other possibilities that might work well within your practice. A successful law firm has a marketing plan that encompasses several different channels, each with potentially different benefits for your firm.

Get comfortable with technology

Lawyers might actually be one of the last group of professionals to completely move into the digital age and start using digital strategies to attract and retain clients.

I've seen this reluctance first-hand from a national law firm that I expected would consistently be using all digital marketing tools at their disposal. Here's what happened. Back in 2014, I had a small legal job I wanted to outsource, so I hired a partner at this firm to review a document. He only completed a couple of hours of work but, as he had opened a file, I presumed I was now on the firm's database. That presumption was correct because two years later I received a newsletter email from them. *Two years* later! It took two years for them to touch base with me. That's two years of missed opportunity. This is a big national firm with more than twenty people in their marketing department in Melbourne alone. I couldn't believe it.

Clearly they had been focusing all of their efforts on offline methods to attract and retain clients. They had somehow forgotten the importance of using technology to stay 'front of mind' for existing clients. The worst part about this is that marketing to their existing client base is something that can easily be automated with a client relationship management tool, a tool they probably already have. It doesn't even require a lot of time or effort.

While I might sound quite negative about this, it's actually a very positive thing to have discovered. Every minute these big law firms don't utilise technology to their advantage is an opportunity for you to get ahead. Remember, you don't need to be large in size these days to have a large presence in the market.

If big law firms want to focus their efforts on offline marketing channels, let them. Over time, advances in the use of technology in law will mean those firms will become more and more irrelevant because their marketing efforts are largely not scalable. It's therefore important to consider how online marketing channels and tools can work for your practice.

Consider your ideal client. Where do they spend time online? Are they spending time on Google, on Facebook or LinkedIn? If so, that's where you need to be.

Where you look for clients obviously depends on the nature of your business and the services that you offer but, whichever service you offer, a digital strategy will put you in good stead, so it's very important to get comfortable with technology so that you can meet potential customers both offline and online.

Get a great website

In this day and age, every law firm owner is aware that a solid and functional website is a necessity.

Unfortunately, the process of developing a website is a minefield of potential mistakes, wasted money and wasted time. I've seen many law firm websites that are so bad that they actually have the potential to affect the law firm's brand in a very negative way.

These days one of your first interactions with a prospective client is likely to be online. Perhaps a friend has recommended you to them, perhaps they've read an article you've written, or perhaps they saw some marketing material you've developed. They check you out online – after all, don't you do that to others? Your website will tell them a lot about whether or not you're the right lawyer for them, so it's important to take time to think about what your website is portraying to the market.

Consider how you want to design your website. Do you want to be be professional and modern, or traditional and functional? Do you want to appear bigger than you actually are or are you happy to come across as a small business?

Whether you're getting your first website developed or replacing your existing one, it's important that you consider all elements of your website before you go live. Some considerations might include what message you're trying to send, how you want the user to engage with your website, how much content you want to make available, whether you want additional features that allow you to engage directly with your client (e.g. live chat), how you will measure engagement on the site, what platform you use and whether you want the ability to make changes yourself. The list goes on.

While it may seem overwhelming, getting the right developer on board with the right experience will put you in good stead. If they are good, they will ask you these questions and help you to launch a website that reflects your end goals. Great developers are also great at strategy and design, so ensure you do your research before hiring a developer to build your site. If you can afford it, choose a team that includes a web developer and a web designer and let them work together to give you specialised advice in both areas.

Create great content

Creating great content is the cornerstone of any successful website and there are several reasons for that. By content, I don't just mean writing legal articles and uploading them onto your site. This type of content is very important, of course, but it's not the only type of content you should focus on. Content also includes how you choose to express yourself on the most visited pages of your website, such as your home page or your 'About Us' page. If the content on these pages isn't high quality, it's unlikely the user will go past those pages to read your more detailed content (unless you're directing traffic directly to specific blogs aimed at a specific market ... but more on that later).

Regardless of how talented your graphic designer or website developer is or how much money you spend driving traffic to your site, if you don't take the time to develop reliable, well-written and useful content, you are unlikely to keep people on your site long enough to consider contacting you.

But remember, before you publish any content on your site, make sure you edit and proofread your content. As obvious as this sounds, you only get one chance to make that first impression. Treat your website as if it were a document to be presented to court. Make it perfect.

As you consider the content you want to create, have a think about your end user. What is your prospective client's experience when they visit your website? What are they looking for and how can you make it easy for them to find what they are looking for in as few clicks as possible? How do they like to receive and engage with your content? Are they interested in long articles with lots of text? Probably not. So think about how they might receive complex legal information in simple, easy to comprehend, ways. Perhaps you can use short articles with dot points and links for further information. Or perhaps you deliver the information in the form of videos. The point here is to view your own business from the mindset of a prospective client who is already overwhelmed by the necessity to contact a lawyer. Make it easy for them to understand who you are and choose you.

You'll also need to consider the following when creating a plan for your content delivery:

- how will you organise the content on your site for maximum value?
- how much content do you want to provide on the site versus in person?
- how often would you like to update your content?
- how easy is it for you to update your website content?
- how interactive do you want your website content to be?

All of these questions are important when planning your website content strategy. There are many more questions to ask, but if you answer the above questions, you'll be ahead of most lawyers from day one. Why is this? Generally speaking, most lawyers don't pay attention to the user experience or what the user of their site wants to achieve from their content. Instead, they pay attention to how they want to demonstrate their knowledge in a particular area of law. They focus on the wrong person.

Once you've got some ideas about your content strategy, start mapping out how you want users to engage with your content and how you'd like the content delivered. Quite simply, create a flow chart that shows how you want your website to function. When you click on 'X', where do you want the user to go? If you map out the basic structure of how you'd like your website to work and how you'd like the content to be delivered, you can deliver that information to your developer and save a lot of time and money.

However you choose to create and deliver your content, it's important to remember how very impatient people can be when looking for answers on the internet. No one wants to wade through millions of words or click through five or six different pages to find the answer. Therefore, any content you provide in a written format should provide short, concise paragraphs with short sentences and bullet points. Videos are even better.

Videos

Video content marketing is becoming a popular way to connect with your ideal client base. In fact, the majority of the top brands around the world now embed their own YouTube videos into their websites. The reason for this is that video content is much more engaging (there are also search engine benefits to having YouTube videos on your site).

On average, people are about ten times more likely to engage with video content than they would on blogs. It's a very powerful content marketing strategy and one that few lawyers use.

If you've made the brave decision to use videos on your website (or maybe even your Facebook page), you'll need to make sure they have a purpose and are not mind-numbingly boring or over-legalistic. You want to grab the user's attention and give them short, to the point information in plain language.

If you're not comfortable on camera just yet but you'd like to use video content, you could get an 'explainer' video created. These are normally short videos with characters or whiteboard drawings that explain what your business does. Originally explainer videos were once used to explain complex services or products, but now they are used commonly to provide a snapshot of your value proposition in under two minutes. They are a lot more popular in certain countries in the world (like the United States) than others, but if it's this or nothing, I'd choose this.

If you're comfortable on camera, one of your first videos could be a brand-storytelling video. These videos are a great way to communicate directly to your clients what you and your business are about. You might want to share your values, your vision, what you're trying to achieve and how you can help your clients. Importantly, they are a very useful way to share your 'why'. It's effectively a trust-building exercise with your potential client base.

Other people use videos on customised landing pages, so that the content you're providing to your client base is very targeted and aimed at boosting conversions. For instance, you might have a landing page dedicated to family law, and on that landing page you might have a video that addresses the three most commonly asked questions in family law. The video therefore helps answer your prospective client's questions, whilst simultaneously demonstrating your expertise, raising your credibility and helping you connect with the prospective client.

Whatever the purpose of your video-marketing strategy, make sure that your content is relatable, easy to understand and easily accessible. Then share that content across all of your social media platforms.

SEO
You may have heard people talk about SEO. SEO stands for 'search engine optimisation'. Put simply, SEO is just a way to make your website more visible in search results. By optimising your content, it tells the search engines how to find your content when someone is looking for the answers that you're providing.

For example, let's say you write a blog about the legal aspects of how to start a business and you upload that blog onto your website. Holly comes along and she wants to start her own business but is not sure what documents she needs in place before she launches that business. She types into an internet search engine: 'what legal documents do I need to start a business?' Luck has it that you have written a blog on this very topic and you have optimised that blog so the search engine has found your page and has put it right in front of Holly who is looking for some legal guidance. Your content is relevant to Holly and she spends time on your site, looking at your blog, understanding your experience and learning to trust you and what you have to say. She may even pick up the phone or email you for more information or a consultation.

The best part of SEO is that, unlike other forms of search engine marketing that can be very expensive, it's free! You can easily learn to optimise your webpages and your blogs. There's even a plug in you can get for most websites that shows you exactly how to do it. For those with bigger budgets who want a bigger online presence, there are also marketing companies who can optimise all of your current and past content for you.

SEM or 'paid' searches

SEM simply stands for 'search engine marketing', and is often used as a way to make your website more visible in search results through the use of paid advertising.

Adwords is probably the most common form of paid SEM at the moment. Most of you will be familiar with Adwords, but for those who aren't, it's simply the advertising platform used through Google that allows you to pay to have your ad for your business appear near or at the top of the page when people type certain words or phrases into Google.

Unlike SEO, you pay Google for this advertising every time your ad appears or every time it's clicked on (depending on your settings). You have to bid for a position on the page relevant to a particular word or phrase (a keyword). The more competitive the keyword, the more you'll have to bid to appear higher on the list of search results. The higher you are on the search results, the more likely the prospective client will click on your ad.

For example, say you're a family lawyer and you want to advertise your divorce services. You choose a keyword or phrase relevant to divorce, and you bid on that keyword or phrase. Now when someone searches for that keyword or phrase, a link to your website comes up.

One huge benefit about Adwords as opposed to SEO is that you can measure exactly what your return on investment is. Google will tell you exactly what you spent to get that customer to your site. Provided you have the right tools set up to track leads, you can determine what your client acquisition costs are for Adwords (i.e. Adwords spend × conversion rate). This information feeds into your marketing spend and your decisions about which keywords to target for maximum profitability.

You can also broaden or narrow your audience, depending on your ideal client base, and of course one of the main benefits is that Adwords can help you increase your client base almost immediately (as opposed to SEO which can take time to see results).

Adwords can be switched on and off, according to busier or quieter times of your working life. You can also set a particular budget for your Adwords campaigns, so you don't have to worry about spending more than you've planned to spend.

If you're trying to break into a crowded market, Adwords can be quite effective. For instance, your competitors may only be using SEO, if anything, so, by utilising an Adwords campaign, you're more likely to have your business show up in search results ahead of your competitors.

You might say that your competitors are already using Adwords, so there's no point. I would disagree with this. If your competitors are there, you need to be there too. Don't let them eat all of the pie!

If you've decided you'd like to try SEO or SEM (or both), I'd recommend hiring a professional to create and manage your campaigns. By using an appropriate expert, you can have a much more targeted and effective campaign. If you have the time or the inclination, I'd also recommend trying to understand how both SEO and SEM work on a broad level. This will help you better understand and instruct the people managing your account.

Networking

Most lawyers I know are quite experienced in the art of networking. Whether or not they enjoy networking is another matter. Lawyers are good at this because they understand that people want to buy legal services from people they know, like and trust. After all, lawyers aren't really selling law, they're selling peace of mind.

Your personal and professional networks are very valuable and are highly linked to your success. At a minimum, they enable you to build rapport and create word-of-mouth referrals. They can also help you raise your profile through collaborations and speaking opportunities.

Even if you're the smartest digital marketer in the world, networking should always form part of your marketing initiative. Basically, if you're not paying attention to building and maintaining networks and relationships, sales will often start to decline. Once sales are down, it can take several months and a lot of effort to build them back up.

As a lawyer you are probably well versed in the importance of networking, so I'll keep this brief and give you just a couple of tips that might help.

First, when selecting which networking event to attend, choose one where your target market will be. This might sound obvious but it's important to think laterally. If your target market is accountants, show up at an accounting conference. While the conference material may not be entirely relevant, the audience is. You may even be the only lawyer there in a room full of accountants. Perfect!

Second, before every networking event, try to get a hold of the guest list from the organiser. This saves you a lot of time because you can target exactly who you want to speak with at the event, and spend your time locating those people and connecting with them. Most people attend networking events and speak with whomever approaches them. This can be a big waste of time. Your time is valuable, so it's important to have some goals in place. The goal might be to meet five new quality contacts, or it might be to progress discussions regarding a business deal with a prospective client.

Whatever you do, the most important tip I can give you regarding networking is to always focus on listening to what the person you are speaking with is saying. Be interested, ask questions, get to know them on a personal level. It's incredible how much people like to talk about themselves, and how high of an opinion they form of you if you let them. Remember, networking is not about making a sale, it's about building relationships. If in addition to listening you can also help them by adding some value, even better.

After all that listening, it will be important to remember some of the detail so that next time you see them you can connect more easily. One great tip is to put something about that person on the back of the business card they give you. Try writing down something that will trigger your memory. Imagine seeing that person again and saying, 'How is your son, George, going at university?' or 'Hey, you know that golf club you wanted? I saw it the other day on sale. Here are the details'. That level of detail really stays with people and keeps you 'front of mind'.

Speaking opportunities

Most networking events you attend these days have a guest speaker. Speaking at an event, whether it's a networking event or a conference, is a very effective way to build your profile and position yourself as an expert in a particular area of law.

Most lawyers have an innate fear of public speaking. I know I certainly do. But the more I do it, the better I get and the more comfortable I feel. If this is a fear of yours, perhaps start small and go from there. Choose a small networking event where there might only be twenty people and pitch to the organiser of that event a talk that you'd like to give their audience that would bring them a lot of value. You'd be surprised how many event organisers are looking for speakers. This will start to build your profile slowly and will help you build your confidence.

The benefits of obtaining speaking opportunities are numerous. At a minimum, they help you raise your profile and stand out as an expert. When your clients (or other lawyers for that matter) see you as an expert, they're much more likely to consider working with you. On top of this, you become visible to multitudes of people who may want to partner with you (not in the traditional partnership sense but in the business sense) and you often get to distribute your marketing materials to the entire room.

When you are granted a speaking opportunity, it's important to make the most of it. Publicise it across your social media platforms, provide valuable content to the audience and share some interesting insights. Most importantly, target your pitch to the audience's experience level and interests.

Have you ever noticed that engaging speakers often have very little information on their PowerPoint presentations? This is so they can engage with the audience directly and speak to the content that they know, rather than reading from slides or notes. Steve Jobs is a great example.

Whether it's at a local community group or at a big conference, every single opportunity to speak to many rather than to one is a chance to position yourself as an expert. If you're unsure where to look for speaking opportunities, have a look at other lawyers in your specialty area and see where they might be speaking.

It's also important to look at your local business networking groups and approach members of those groups to let them know you're interested in speaking opportunities.

Of course when you're approaching these organisations, be very clear about the areas you're willing to speak on. Ideally, you should be only speaking on your subject matter expertise in your particular niche. Try to be as inspiring and engaging as you can. After all, you want people to listen to you and hopefully refer you to other people for more speaking opportunities.

Partnerships

As a lawyer, you're operating in a highly competitive environment so it's important to look for new ways to stay ahead of your competitors. One way to do this is to forge strategic partnerships with other businesses. After all, we know that one of the biggest mistakes business owners make is to try to do everything by themselves.

By forming strategic business partnerships, you're effectively agreeing to enter into an arrangement that aims to help both of your businesses achieve more success. The biggest benefit of strategic partnerships is that they can often help you grow your business quite quickly and for very little, if any, monetary outlay.

Most lawyers are actually quite savvy about the benefits of partnerships. The idea of course is to find a complementary business so you can refer clients to one another. Take a business lawyer and an accountant who works with SMEs for example. Most of the clients the accountant has will at some point need some legal advice, and most of the lawyer's clients will probably need accounting advice. A partnership here is a win-win because both parties are able to increase their client base and thus increase revenue without increasing their marketing spend.

When you're reflecting on who might be your strategic partner, have a think about who your ideal client sees before and after they need you. A property lawyer, for example, is acutely aware that vendors of property see a real estate agent before selling their house. Once they've decided they want to sell their house, they need a contract of sale to be drawn up, so real estate agents are a perfect referral source. After the sale, they may need insurance for their new home, so you could refer them to an insurance broker, and so on, and so on. If you start to get creative about strategic partnerships, you'll start to see how many opportunities exist right in front of you.

Once you have a list of potential strategic partners, try to clarify exactly what you have to offer and what you're expecting in return. Are you able to send referrals back to them? If not, are they expecting a monetary referral fee for referrals they send to you? Before you agree on any strategic partnerships, it should be clear what each partner could potentially bring to the table and whether or not that is in line with the way you wish to run your firm.

It's also important to ensure your strategic partnerships operate in a way that will reflect well on you and your business. The best strategic partners are often those who have the same ideal client, and also have similar visions, values and goals as you.

You may need to trial several different strategic partners before finding the right ones, but once you do find the right strategic partnerships, you will have a competitive advantage and a way to grow your business exponentially at very little cost, if any.

Referrals

Referrals are obviously linked to the idea of strategic partnerships, and they are certainly one of the most valuable assets a lawyer can have. Being a lawyer is so often about creating a relationship of trust, so being referred by someone is a great start to building trust with a prospective client.

One of the biggest benefits of referrals is that the conversion rates (i.e. turning that referral into a client) from referrals are often quite high, presumably because the client has already removed any major objections about trust, simply through being referred by someone they know. The other main benefit, of course, is that there are no acquisition costs.

Lawyers are very aware of these benefits and often focus on building referrals. Some lawyers are much better than others at doing this. What makes some lawyers good at this and some lawyers not so good? I think it comes down to taking action and asking for what you want.

One of the main obstacles lawyers have when trying to build a referral-based marketing channel is that they actually don't ask for referrals. They expect that if they provide a good service, they will automatically get referrals. That might be the case sometimes, but often a referral is something that you need to ask for. You'd be surprised how many people are willing to send you referrals if they know you'd like to receive them.

People often don't ask for referrals for a couple of reasons:

- they don't want to be seen as someone who's desperate for work; and/or
- they're concerned about bothering their clients or receiving a 'no' in response.

This makes absolutely no sense to me. It's important to be able to ask for what you want, and who in the world, successful or not, would not want to receive referrals? They can ultimately become a huge source of clients and help you grow your business quickly.

Often, successful firms also reward clients and staff for referring work to them. A reward can be in a form that's comfortable to you. It might be as simple as a phone call or an email to say 'Thank you for thinking of us'. Or it might be a cash incentive or a bottle of wine sent in the mail.

Whichever way you reward or recognise a referral, it's important to do so.

Reviews

Online reviews from people who have used your service can be just as powerful, if not more powerful, than direct referrals. These days, the majority of your prospective customers will be looking at your online footprint, including online reviews, to help determine whether or not to contact you. Several great reviews of your service and experience will take them one step further towards becoming a client.

One of the major obstacles for people when they want online reviews is that they don't actually know how to ask for one. Alternatively, people are afraid of receiving bad reviews online, so they don't ask for any. As a lawyer, you will at some point have a client who is not satisfied. That's OK; it's impossible to make everyone happy. Don't let it stop you from getting some incredible reviews from the hundreds of clients who have loved your service. The most effective way of combatting or reducing the impact of a negative review is to get many positive reviews about your service.

In terms of how to obtain online reviews, you simply need to ask for them. You can do this in an automated way by incorporating the request into one of your existing processes. For instance, if you send receipts to clients by email, generate a link to add to those receipts so your clients have the option of giving you a review. This is a particularly good time to ask for a review as they have recently used your service and you are still in their thoughts. The link can be to LinkedIn, to Google, to your Facebook page, wherever you like. Importantly, try to send client reviews to a place where other clients may be looking for your services. If you get clients through LinkedIn, start asking for LinkedIn reviews.

If building a process to ask for reviews sounds like an overwhelming task, contact your five best customers and personally ask them for a review by email or phone. They may wish to do this in the form of a testimonial which you can put on your website (with their permission) and distribute through your social media channels.

Remember not to ask the client to give you a 'good' review. It's important the reviews come across as honest and authentic, so that means no set wording or any suggestions about what they should say. They need to speak from their personal experience.

Once you've got a few reviews, make sure you acknowledge and respond to them online, whether good or bad. This demonstrates that you appreciate and respond well to feedback and that you care about your service delivery.

Building relationships

Every successful law firm owner knows that the success of their business is rooted in their ability to build relationships with clients. It doesn't matter if those relationships are in person or online; it's about getting to know your clients and your clients getting to know you and how you can help solve their legal problems.

Relationship building is important not only for clients, but also for suppliers, staff and strategic partners – basically, everyone with whom your firm engages on a day-to-day basis. When you have tight deadlines and budgets to meet, it's these relationships that will guide you through the tumultuous times.

Let's also not underestimate the importance of business relationships with other business owners, including lawyers. Even if they don't provide complementary services, sharing your challenges and your wins with these people can yield useful insights.

By building relationships with your competitors, you can actually gain a lot more useful information than if you refused to speak with them. If you get to know exactly what other lawyers do and who their target market is, you'll discover that most other lawyers probably aren't competitors. You may service a different area of law or have different target markets. These people can actually be a hidden source of referrals. After all, think about how many clients contact you whom you can't actually help. Perhaps you're a business lawyer and one of your business clients has a family-law matter. If you have built a relationship with a family lawyer, you can refer that client on with an expectation that the family lawyer will refer business clients to you. In fact, even other business lawyers may be a good source of referrals. I see this often where a client wants to sell a business. The purchaser will also need a lawyer, and it can't be you, so you may choose to refer the purchaser to another business lawyer. It's a win-win.

Let rainmakers lead

Most lawyers are familiar with the term 'rainmaker'. It's most commonly attributed to the lawyer that has the ability to go out, form new relationships with clients and bring new clients into the firm. Rainmakers are few and far between in law firms, but they are often promoted quickly, even without superior technical skills. They're very good at two things: building relationships and closing the sale.

The rainmaker is the person who always seems to be able to work the room to the best of their ability, leaving the event with at least a handful of contacts that may lead to work. They are 'big picture' people, so they often work best when paired with detail-oriented people.

What I find interesting is that lawyers often think that they are either a 'rainmaker' or a 'worker' and that it is very difficult to be both. Generally, this view is based on beliefs around personality differences (i.e. introversion and extroversion) that are fixed.

However, I believe that any lawyer can go from being a great 'worker' bee to a great 'rainmaker'. It takes a bit of practice, and requires letting go of fears around marketing, profile raising and networking. It's a mindset shift and it may not feel natural at first.

True rainmakers value relationships, build relationships and maintain and nurture them over time. Rainmakers aren't just looking out for themselves; they are often very focused and attentive to others. They connect. They are genuinely interested in people and they are problem solvers. Their focus is not just the legal challenge, but rather the challenge of finding a holistic solution for a client.

If you don't consider yourself to be a 'natural' rainmaker, don't worry; just start taking small steps. Remember to keep networking, think about the value you can give your clients (without requiring anything in return), start really listening to clients when they talk about problems, and try for the most part to enjoy your interactions with people and form relationships.

How technically proficient you are as a lawyer only gets you so far. You must be able to form trusted advisor relationships with your clients in order to successfully grow your business.

Google Alerts

Regardless of whether you are yet to have an online presence, remember that many of your competitors do. One way to keep ahead of the curve and understand exactly what's happening in your niche marketplace is to use what's called Google Alerts. It's one of Google's hidden gems and it's such a powerful tool to be able to understand exactly what's happening in your market and how your competitors are performing. In addition, it allows you to keep track of when other people are talking about you or your service on the internet and what they're saying about you.

Setting up Google Alerts is as simple as selecting what you'd like to be alerted to. This could be terms such as your business name, your personal name, or perhaps your biggest competitor's business name. Just select how often and in which way you'd like to be alerted.

For instance, I have a strong interest in fixed-fee legal services, so I have a Google Alert set up that alerts me to articles or news relating to fixed-fee legal services. I also have alerts set up relating to my main competitors. This enables me to understand when they have been published online through media outlets. You may also wish to set up alerts for your clients, perhaps for some of your bigger clients, so you can keep abreast in what's happening in their businesses. Then you can be proactive and touch base with clients when you're alerted to something happening in their business.

It certainly makes clients feel valued if you're up to date on what's happening in their world.

Newsjacking

Newsjacking is a term used for taking breaking news stories and injecting your ideas and angles into the story in order to generate media coverage for your practice. The beautiful thing about newsjacking is that it's open to anyone, any player in the market, who's observant and quick to react to news. Richard Branson was a big fan of this tactic in his early days with Virgin airlines.

Google Alerts can be used to bring to your attention things that are happening in the media that you may wish to newsjack. Newsjacking has become an increasingly popular method for brands to be able to gain visibility and media coverage for their business in a very cost effective way.

If you're intending to newsjack, it's wise to have a bit of a plan before you leap into action. Obviously newsjacking requires quick action, but it's important that any action you take will ultimately benefit your business and show your practice in a positive light. Done poorly, it can bring a lot of negative attention to your practice.

It's important to keep it relevant, so it needs to be an obvious link between the news and how your brand would relate to that news. Only get involved if there's a very relevant and respectful link between the news and your practice. Most importantly, be quick. If you see something on the evening news, you will need to get something in the form of a media release out to journalists prior to six am the next morning.

Lastly, be very clear about the goal for newsjacking. Are you wanting people to visit your website? Call you? Sign up to your newsletter? Try to be very clear about what you want and how you will measure your success from the newsjacking before you get started.

Spend money to make money

We all know the common saying that you need to spend money to make money, but how does this apply to your practice? Most firms run on a very tight budget, particularly if you're new to the market. As such, there's an inclination to try to get as much as you can for nothing.

Of course there are certain products, services and information that you'll be able to obtain for free that will help you improve and run your practice more effectively. However, the old saying that 'you get exactly what you pay for' rings true.

Try to take a blended approach. You can certainly try free activities to market your practice such as blog writing or networking events (although remember there is a time cost here too), but in order to truly grow, it's important to invest in yourself. A great investment these days is in education around digital marketing and social media, mainly because most lawyers are not doing amazing things in this space, so if you know what you're doing you can easily gain a competitive advantage.

Of course, whenever you spend money, it's important to understand the return on investment and to measure whether or not that's working for you.

Measure everything

Speaking of measuring results, understanding your return on investment is crucial. At first it might feel counter-intuitive because you have to stop the action that is intended to generate further business in order to reflect and appropriately measure whether or not that action is working for you, but stick with it.

The decisions you make about which marketing activities you undertake can mean a huge difference to your bottom line. As most lawyers are acutely aware, time or money (or both) are often in short supply, so by measuring your marketing channels to ensure their effectiveness allows you to prioritise the most effective channels, ultimately saving you time and money.

Measuring activities allows you to make informed decisions about your marketing strategies.

Whether you capture this data in fancy online marketing tools or you write it down in a book doesn't matter, provided of course that you can collect and analyse that data to see whether it's serving you. If you have a web presence, Google Analytics is a fantastic tool because it's free and enables you to see where your visitors are coming from when they land on your website and what they're doing once they land on your website.

For instance, it can tell you how many people have visited your website in a given time, how they found your website, what they looked at, how much time they spent there and what actions they took.

If you do online marketing, A/B testing is also a common methodology to experiment with different messages and see which ones are resonating with your audience. Then you can make a decision about which marketing messages to stick with and which ones to stop.

If you don't have much of an online presence, you can measure your data the old-fashioned way by tracking what type of enquiries you're receiving, where they came from, whether or not they converted into client, what the profit margin was and what their feedback was...the list goes on. Every bit of data you track gives you insight into how you're attracting, converting and retaining clients. At an absolute minimum, this is the basic information you need for your business.

If you're already across the basics, consider investing in a comprehensive CRM that can track and analyse data in seconds.

Remember, not all marketing channels are equal, and if not tracked and measured appropriately, you can waste a lot of time and a lot of money. So it's important to spend the time understanding which channels are most effective for reaching your target market.

Chapter 4

Do You Make It Easy For Them To Say Yes?

"Try not to become a person of success, but try to become a person of value."

Albert Einstein

Believe it or not, your prospective clients really do want to say 'yes', but they really don't want to be 'sold' to. No one likes a hard sale, no one. So how do you get your prospective clients to move along the sales pipeline to get to 'yes' without being pushy? The good news is that it's easier than you think. There are a lot of ways you can influence a prospective client's purchasing decisions without explicitly selling to them, so let's take a look at a few.

Demonstrate credibility

Your prospective clients are more likely to buy from you if they see you as possessing unique credibility. It's obvious, right? Every lawyer I've ever met wants to be credible. But what is credibility? Credibility for lawyers is often closely linked to being considered a 'trusted advisor'. That is, an advisor who has the knowledge, skill and ability to help clients solve legal problems.

The problem that many lawyers face is that while they have the requisite knowledge, skills and abilities, they often fail to demonstrate this to clients. Either they don't know how to demonstrate their credibility to clients effectively, or they take the view that clients will automatically think they're credible because of their status or position at a law firm. Either way, a failure to adequately demonstrate credibility to your prospective clients at the outset can drastically affect your ability to turn those prospects into clients.

There are a number of ways in which you can demonstrate credibility. The traditional way is to talk with prospective clients face-to-face (or on the phone) about your legal experience, other similar cases you've worked on and, importantly, how you feel you could help them quickly and easily resolve their issue. Ideally, you could also give them a lot of value by giving them a complimentary consultation to discuss their matter. The more value you give at the outset, the more you have an opportunity to demonstrate your skill set. All of this should be done before discussing fees.

While it's important to establish your credibility when a prospective client is sitting in front of you, the best time to establish credibility is actually before you get them in your office. If your prospective clients already see you as credible before they meet you, you have a much higher chance of converting them into paying clients once they're sitting in front of you because they're already mostly sold on you. In fact, if you do this well, you can even dispense with the need for face-to-face meetings and simply advise clients virtually, having never met them.

Establishing credibility with your target audience can be achieved by utilising a number of proven strategies. Most of the strategies are in some way linked to demonstrating your competence through content marketing.

So how can you start to demonstrate your competence? The first step is to know which area of law you're most competent in. Even if you have experience in a number of different areas, there is generally one area of law where your expertise is stronger. This area, otherwise known as your niche, will be what you'll focus on.

The primary goal is for your target market to see you as the expert in that area of law. To become the expert, you'll need to start getting comfortable with content marketing. By developing and sharing relevant and interesting information that is directly linked to your niche, you will start to become known for your deep understanding and expertise in that area. You might develop content in the form of a book, a blog, a guide or a conference paper.

Whatever form your content takes, be sure to develop that content for your target market and put that information directly in front of your target market. I know this sounds simple and logical, but here's some big mistakes I see lawyers make all the time:

- they develop content that only lawyers can understand
- they present the content to lawyers, not to their target market
- they create amazing content but don't share it.

Have a think about who your client is, what they need to know and where they spend time. If that's Facebook, guess what? You need to get a business Facebook page and share your content on Facebook. If that's LinkedIn, create a post and share it with all of your contacts. The better the content, the more likely it will be shared and liked and the more exposure you will get. (Hint: people like sharing content that makes them look smart).

In terms of the type of content you create, ensure:

- it's not too long
- that you use lots of subheadings
- that you use plain language
- that you demonstrate the problem and then the solution.

Clients want solutions, not large amounts of hard-to-read text or multiple references to case law – or Latin. Please, no Latin! The more you demonstrate that you understand what they need and want, the more likely they will see you as someone who can help them.

If you want to become the expert in your field, it's not a time to be bashful. Recognise the achievements you've already made in your business and your career and then put them front and centre for all to see. It's important to be proud of your achievements and allow them to promote your credibility. Whenever I'm on a top 30 lawyers list or top 8 Women in Legal Technology list I share it with the world. Why not? I've worked hard to get here.

Website lead generation

Website lead generation is an internet marketing term that refers to generating prospective customers or enquiries through the internet. Leads can be generated for a number of purposes, but ultimately the goal is to convert that lead *when they're ready to buy*.

Leads build your contact list, and contact lists are extremely valuable in and of themselves. I see many lawyers ignoring this, assuming that the only purpose of website lead generation is to generate a lead who will buy right there and then. If not, they're often discarded as a time waster. This couldn't be further from the truth. Leads are valuable because, if they're properly nurtured and if you demonstrate your credibility well, they can turn into work down the track, or even serve as a good referral source.

Generally a lead is considered to be the contact information of the prospect (name, email, phone number), including in some instances an idea of their interest in a specific product or service. There are lots of different types of lead generation, but we're talking specifically about online lead generation from your website.

Entire books could be written about lead generation, so most lawyers feel overwhelmed. They know that they need better qualified and more consistent leads to grow their practice, but they're not sure where to start when it comes to the online world.

A good place to start is to have an online presence, and ideally a website (though a website actually isn't even needed these days to generate leads…but that's another story). Once you have a website, you need to drive traffic to your website, and ideally 'qualified' traffic, meaning people who are searching for legal solutions.

There are many different strategies for driving traffic to your website so let's take one example of a basic strategy and follow it through the process.

Let's say your target market is separated women who are looking for a divorce. You might create an amazing blog post on divorce, post it on your blog and share that content on Facebook either with your friends (hoping it will be shared) or through Facebook ads that target separated women in your area.

Success! Mary, thirty-seven, clicks on your blog and gets directed to your website where you have the full text of the blog. She finds the information useful. To the right of the blog post, she sees information about who you are, and that you're offering a free family-law consultation. To get a consultation, she must send her details through to you. After you get her details, you organise a complimentary consultation in which you can show her how you can solve her legal problem.

Now obviously this is a very basic strategy but it is one that works well. The main points are:

- the content was useful to her as it helped her understand how the divorce process works
- you had a dedicated landing page on your website for family law (you stayed relevant)
- you demonstrated a little bit about who you are and you offered her something of value
- you made it easy for her to accept your offer.

What you offer in exchange for her information could be anything of perceived value. It could be a cheat sheet for how to go through a divorce, maybe a flow chart about the court process, or perhaps a newsletter sign-up (though these are less valuable these days). Whatever it is, it needs to be relevant and valuable to your audience. Free consultations are great, but if they're not ready for a consultation yet, you run the risk of losing the lead. For this reason, you may like to have a couple of options on your landing page so the prospect can pick the offer that is of most value to them.

It really is worth taking the time (at a minimum once a year) to consider your website lead generation strategy. The better your strategy, the better your conversion rate, and ultimately the better your revenue.

Once you start getting the leads in the door, it's important to record them and what happens to them so you understand your conversion rate (i.e. how many leads convert into paying clients). Bear in mind that most websites convert at a rate of 10% or under (in fact 10% is actually very good these days), so not every visitor will turn into a client.

If you want to start increasing the traffic to your site, you could try some or all of the following:

- create and share more content
- run ads to your site
- get an SEO specialist
- get other sites to mention your site (backlinks).

Once you have traffic here are some ideas to capture the lead:

- have dedicated landing pages
- keep them on your site longer with videos
- have opt-in boxes on most pages
- have contact information at the top of each page
- have a 'get a quote' page
- have multiple lead magnets (ebook, cheat sheet etc.)
- install 'Live Chat' to speak with clients directly online.

Once you have the lead, ensure you nurture that lead via email. There are a lot of client relationship management tools out there these days that help you to nurture leads in an automatic and relevant way.

For any lawyer looking to compete in this day and age, it's crucial that they get across even the basics of online lead generation. For

Legally Yours, 90% of our leads are online and I wouldn't have it any other way.

Create a call to action

A 'call to action' is quite literally a call to your prospective client to take some form of action. On a website it might be an image or text that pops up that prompts your website visitors to do something. The action that you require the prospect to take could be anything from downloading an ebook, to getting a will done, to attending an event.

A call to action is effectively a trigger that informs someone to take that next logical step in the direction that you want him or her to go. Clearly, the call to action needs to be so compelling and persuasive that you engage the user and get them to take that next step.

Let's take the example of an email marketing campaign to your current business-law clients. Perhaps there has been a development in privacy law that they need to know about and you've created a cheat sheet so they can understand the issue in under five minutes.

You want them to download the cheat sheet so they can assess whether they need to update their privacy policy, and if they do, you hope they will call you because you're clearly already across the changes.

In this instance you may create a call to action in the following way:

1. Send them an email letting them know about the changes and making it clear why they should download your cheat sheet (i.e. the value of getting across the changes in five minutes rather than sifting through the internet to figure it out).
2. Create a sense of urgency by telling them that the changes may mean that their current privacy policy might be ineffective.

3. Make it easy to get the information by telling them to click on the button in the email, enter their name and email and the cheat sheet will automatically be delivered to them in minutes.

4. Once they have the information, follow them up with an email asking if it was useful and if they would like a review of their privacy policy (perhaps do this for free or for a nominal fee as you may get drafting work out of it).

Once they download the information you will now have a list of clients who have already used your services who may be interested in another service, a review of their current privacy policy with potentially a new privacy policy.

You can also have this cheat sheet on your website for download in exchange for names and email addresses.

When creating a call to action try to ensure:

- the button or text is in a contrasting colour that stands out
- if on a website, the button is above the fold
- the call to action is stated in a simple and clear way
- there is a specified landing page to enter in lead information.

Once you understand the value of using a call to action, you will start to see them everywhere around you!

Forget 'what' and focus on 'why'

One of the biggest mistakes I see lawyers make every day, particularly during presentations, is that they focus on the 'what' or the 'how' rather than the 'why' of what they're doing. Of course your audience needs to understand what you do and how you might work, but believe me, your audience is actually more interested in what your 'why' is.

By understanding your 'why', clients or prospective clients can become inspired by the passion for the work that you do, even if they're not that interested in the work themselves (which, let's face it, most clients aren't). But focusing on the 'why' will establish a context of why your work is so important to you and therefore why it should be important to them. People will identify with your 'why'.

One of the best TED talks I've ever watched is by a man called Simon Sinek, where he talks about the fundamental difference between companies like Apple and other companies. He says that the successful companies always start with 'why'. They ask themselves what the core belief of their business is and why it exists. Only once this question is answered can you talk about how the business operates in the context of fulfilling that core belief, and what the company does to fulfil that core belief.

What Sinek discussed in his TED talk is that most companies actually do their marketing backwards, in that they start from the what, move to the how and often even neglect to demonstrate why they do what they're doing. But once you focus on your why, it becomes the core of your marketing strategy and certainly the driving force behind your business operations.

He uses Apple as an example. If Apple had started backwards by talking about their 'what', they would talk about making computers that are user-friendly, beautifully designed and easy to use. Then they would ask whether you'd like to buy one. Boring! Although these facts about Apple are all true, this is not why people buy Apple products.

In reality, Apple focuses almost entirely on the 'why'. They say, 'With everything we do, we aim to challenge the status quo, we aim to think differently. Our products are user-friendly, beautifully designed and easy to use. We just happen to make great computers. Want to buy one?'

Sinek focuses on the difference between these marketing messages to demonstrate how different they feel and how much more attractive they are to customers who fundamentally share the same beliefs. As Sinek says, people don't buy what you do, they buy why you do it.

Starting with the 'why' makes your law firm flourish against your competitors who have similar expertise and similar capabilities.

Handling objections

Lawyers often encounter objections from prospective clients. Perhaps it's that the legal fees are expensive and they 'can't afford that right now', or perhaps they say they will get around to it but they 'just don't have the time right now'. Sound familiar?

In response to objections, lawyers often shy away, believing objections to be a bad thing or that there's no chance that person will become a client. I believe the opposite to be true. If clients are openly talking about their concerns, it means they're giving you a chance to handle that objection. It actually shows that they are somewhat interested in your service; otherwise, they wouldn't even bother to share their objection with you.

When clients share their objections with you, it's important to view these objections as simply a request for more information, a signal that your prospect is potentially interested in you and that you need to take action and demonstrate value in order to bring that sale to a close.

Here's a simple process to help you understand and resolve your prospective client's objections.

1. Listen to the objection. It's important to allow your prospective client to explain exactly what the issue is and exactly why they don't feel your service is right for them at that point in time. This information gives you very valuable clues on how to handle the objection.
2. Repeat the objection back to your client. Once your prospective client has completed sharing their objection

with you, it's important to engage in active listening techniques by reflecting that information back to them. This shows that you're listening and gives them a chance to clarify if they are incorrect. For example, if a client expresses concern about costs around your services, once they've finished explaining, you might say, 'I understand that you need this particular service, but your primary concern is around costs.'

3. Once you've asked enough questions, restated the objection or clarified it, you've got enough information to be clear about what their real objection is. When you respond to the real objection, it's important to be very clear and keep the response short, honest and to the point. Long-winded responses to the objections very quickly begin to sound insincere.

4. Propose a resolution to overcome that objection and check back in with your prospective client to see whether the proposed solution will satisfy the objection.

Only after you've followed the above steps is it time to take that sale forward.

If money appears to be the main objection, generally it's actually not the problem. The problem is that you haven't demonstrated your value correctly. I can't say this enough, it's not them, it's *you*. It's often the case that the more value you provide, the more that buyer is able to magically find the money to buy that solution from you.

A crucial tip that I learned the hard way is to not engage in any discussions about money too soon. Talking about money too soon will always make the amount sound too high because you generally haven't had the opportunity to demonstrate value yet. Try to delay the money discussion until you've talked about the value that you're able to provide that client. If we increase the perceived value we will decrease the money objections.

Last but not least, make sure that you are dealing with a decision-maker. If they're not the decision-maker, money may actually be a problem for them because you are having the value-based conversation with the wrong person.

Give value to your clients

Speaking of value, value-added selling is a very common sales technique that relies on promoting the inherent value of a product or service.

One of the hardest things about value-based selling is getting your target market to understand the full depth and breadth of everything that your law firm has to offer them. In addition, your firm is now competing with the availability of online legal documentation and downward pressure on fees, so it's more important than ever to be able to add value to your service. If you don't, you're at risk of competing on price and that is not where you want to be, trust me.

One of the best ways to add value to your clients is to provide a level of advice that is more sophisticated, more in depth, more relevant and more valuable to them than that of your competition.

In order to do this, you must have a clear understanding of where your value lies, and you must be willing to share your value with people. For lawyers, the value is often in one or more of the following areas:

- expert knowledge in a specific area of law
- plain language content
- fixed-fee legal services.

If you offered all three of the above, you'll be demonstrating a competitive advantage. Most lawyers have some form of expert knowledge in law, but they rarely have the ability to communicate that knowledge in a way that is palatable to their target market. If you add some price certainty to the mix, you're demonstrating a lot of value.

If you do offer fixed fees, the other way that you may wish to increase the perceived value of your offering is to put together some legal packages. For instance, if a client is buying a house and needs help with conveyancing, they may also need to review their will. You could put both of these services in a package at a slightly lower price than the services being sold separately and offer it as an option when they come to you for the conveyance.

One of the most common complaints about lawyers is how long it takes to turn documents around, so one of the best ways to demonstrate value as a lawyer is to focus on the speed of your service delivery. If you can differentiate yourself by guaranteeing some sort of turnaround time, you may be able to charge full or maximum pricing for this, because it is effectively creating or providing a value-added service.

These ways to add value can be applied to your day-to-day sales activities without too much work. By implementing these strategies, you will avoid having to play the price war. Nobody likes a price war.

Package services up front

As lawyers we are very used to charging by the hour and assuming absolutely no risk on fees. While most lawyers find this incredibly attractive, there is a downside. You only ever get paid for the billable hours that you work. If you're sick or on holiday, you don't get paid. In addition, whether you bill at $300 or $800 an hour, your income is always going to be limited to the number of hours that you're able to work. How can you change that? You can create products out of your services.

The idea of productising your services for most lawyers can be a little bit overwhelming, so let's look at a basic example to get you started. Say you're an estate-planning lawyer and you most commonly draft basic wills for clients. If clients pay you by the hour to prepare a very basic will for them, quite quickly that will can become unaffordable. If clients perceive getting their will done as unaffordable, they are less likely to instruct you to prepare their will for them. So how do you reduce the costs for them, move away from an hourly billing method and still maintain profit? You automate processes and improve efficiencies. This means that you are really clear about the processes involved when drafting a will and how much it costs for a will to be created from start to finish. Most of the time, it should not be you spending the time creating the will. Your time is much better spent reviewing the will before execution.

Here are some tips towards on how you might work more efficiently with some automated processes:

- Create an online template to send to clients where they can input data. Online templates are easily created these days, and having clients enter the data means you can move away from long meetings and data input. The answers to the questions should transfer automatically into your will template so your job is just to review and finalise instructions.

- Make sure you delegate anything that either can't be automated or that doesn't require your high level review. For instance, following up on clients who haven't returned the template.

- Reflect on the questions you are asked most frequently regarding the will creation process and create a FAQs document that can be sent to clients when you send them the template. Put this on your website as well. This will save you time on the phone.

- Create a document that outlines your execution instructions. Send it to clients along with their will so they can review and have the documents executed themselves. If you want to check execution, send a return envelope and ask them to send the will back to you for review. This will mean there's no need for an additional meeting to execute the will. You can then store the will for them if they would like that.

Once you've automated processes and improved efficiencies, you can define exactly how much it costs to produce your will (the product) and how much of a profit margin you can apply to that product. The price of your will really comes down to perceived value to the client as well as market expectations.

By following this process, you move away from hourly rates and towards creating outcomes and products for clients. It takes less of your time and can create better profit margins as your volume can increase and the price point is not determined by how many hours you spend drafting.

Stay in front of mind

In this information age, it's very difficult to remain front of mind for your clients. It requires effort, and those that don't put in the effort are usually forgotten. In order to stand out from the crowd, you need to remain engaged with both your current and prospective clients. Even if they're not in a position to buy from you right now, they certainly might be in the future. If you remain engaged with your clients, you'll be first on their list to call if a legal issue comes up.

One way to stay front of mind is to congratulate your clients or prospective clients on their successes. Perhaps you could congratulate them on work anniversaries through LinkedIn, or perhaps you could send them a personalised birthday card or a message when they get a new job or win a new deal. However you choose to do it, people love to be thought of and recognised, so taking the time to send a personalised message will work in your favour.

Lawyers also hold a wealth of information at their fingertips and, more often than not, this valuable information is not shared. If you're open to sharing your knowledge, a regular legal update can be a very useful way to keep your clients engaged. Whether it takes the form of a newsletter, a blog or a short update, giving clients relevant and valuable information can be quite powerful. This is best managed through automated and personalised email marketing. Basic email marketing systems are very cheap these days, and they can personalise your messages based on a number of defined characteristics (i.e. area of law, regular or prospective client, which lead magnet they have downloaded).

Your information should be subtle, not directly sales-focused, and it should contain valuable information that is engaging and informative. For instance, if you're a family lawyer and you notice that most of your clients ask the same five questions, you could create a blog titled 'The five things you need to know before getting divorced'. The blog would be short and informative with lots of subheadings and an easy-to-follow structure.

Email marketing systems also have a lot of great functionality these days, so you can review the engagement your client base has had with your content. This information helps you understand what is resonating with your audience and what is not. More often than not, it's the information we think is quite basic that resonates well with clients. Remember, they don't have the years of experience working in the law that we do, so we often assume they know more than they do.

Often lawyers are reluctant to do email marketing because they don't want a reputation for spamming clients. Other times, lawyers think that email marketing could potentially alienate clients. We understand that these are common fears, but if you make your content relevant and valuable, your emails become a professional and effective way to attract and retain clients, instead of repelling and alienating them.

Importantly, remember not to send them too often and always include an option to unsubscribe.

Chapter 5

Are You Making The Most Of What You Already Have?

"The biggest risk is not taking any risk ... In a world that's changing really quickly, the only strategy that is guaranteed to fail is not taking risks."

Mark Zuckerberg

Most law firms spend the majority of their efforts trying to win new clients. While it's an obvious way to increase revenue, it's not necessarily the easiest or the smartest method. Usually a blended approach of attracting new clients, treating your current clients well and leveraging your historical client base is the most effective method for increasing revenue.

Maintain and utilise your database

Most lawyers have a long list of existing clients that they haven't stayed in touch with. At best, lawyers take out their biggest clients for lunch or drinks every now and again. Other than that, most lawyers don't really stay in contact with their clients, mainly because they consider their job to have been completed. But without contact, these clients disengage over time. What we know is that disengaged clients are less likely to buy from you again than engaged clients. Luckily, there are easy ways to keep those clients engaged. The easiest way is to have a fantastic client relationship management (CRM) tool that holds all of your client information, and then *use that tool*.

Hopefully, you've been recording all of your clients in a database of some sort since you started operating. If not, it's time to start. Databases (and lists) can be one of the most valuable tools any law firm can have. That's why it still shocks me to see how many law firms, big and small, don't actually utilise their database.

If you manage your database well (or implement a CRM tool to do so), it can give you a wealth of information about your clients: how they engage with you, what they buy, what their average spend is, whether they're repeat clients and so on. One of the great features of most CRMs is that you're able to segment your list of clients between different areas of law. So for instance, if you have a law firm that offers business law, family law and estate-planning law, you can segment those clients into different contact groups, so that when you run marketing campaigns, all of those campaigns are optimised and personalised to those particular segments.

CRMs can also help you personalise your communication with your clients or prospective clients in a way that it could never be personalised before. For instance, you can send personalised emails to people on their birthdays or at holiday times. This can certainly go a long way towards building your relationships and it can make a big difference to how your clients perceive you and your service. This is also a fantastic way to stand out from your competition, as most law firms don't do much, if anything, with the information in their database.

Using a CRM to manage client data and automate communication with your database brings you a competitive edge and, at the very least, helps you level the playing field if you don't have a host of staff maintaining communication with your client base.

Be responsive

If you've been in practice for a while, you've probably got a solid book of clients and regularly see new leads coming in. While that's fantastic news, many lawyers drop their standards quite a lot when their practice is going well. The first thing that seems to go out the window is the level of communication and service they provide to their current clients. Sure, it's easy to be responsive when you're not too busy, but when you have deadlines and documents that are waiting to get out, it can be a little tough to spend the time you need to spend with clients.

What I've found over the years when speaking with clients is that (believe it or not) they do generally understand that you are busy. Most clients don't want to waste your time or tie you up when you have pressing deadlines. Most are quite respectful. But what they hate most of all – their most common complaint – is not hearing back from their lawyer. They want to be updated, to know that you've read their email or that you will get around to the task they need you to do, even if that means it won't be done for a couple of days.

When I speak with lawyers about their levels of responsiveness, they often complain about clients being too demanding or needing responses or answers to things immediately. I think this is slightly off the mark, to be honest. Yes, there are demanding clients but, more often than not, clients just need you or someone from your team to touch base with them to let them know what is going on and when they should expect a reply. They're often feeling anxious because they don't understand the process or what is likely to happen next.

For these reasons, I'd encourage you to be open in your communication and clear about your response times. The clearer and more responsive you are (either directly or via a staff member), the happier your clients will be. Remember, clients come to you because they have a problem that they don't know how to resolve themselves, so they need your guidance, both in terms of the law and in terms of the process. To reduce anxiety levels, clients need to feel you are on top of things, and communicating where you are at with the transaction will certainly ease their anxiety.

While being responsive with your communication will certainly help raise your client's satisfaction with your service, being responsive isn't just about returning client calls and emails. Being responsive these days is also about understanding your customers and responding to their needs in the midst of a changing market.

It's important to ensure that your firm reflects on and responds to the changing market conditions. In my experience most law firms either:

- ignore market conditions
- acknowledge market conditions but do nothing about them
- say they are adapting to changes to the market (and innovating) but don't actually create much change.

How do you know what's changing and how to respond to those changes? Ask your clients! Get some data from the people that use your services and/or that of other firms regularly. What do they want or need? What are they not getting? If you do this, you will be light years ahead of most firms who think that if they keep doing what they've always done, they will be fine.

Being responsive also means being proactive and not waiting for clients to reach out and let you know about legal problems that they might have. Reaching out on a regular basis means that you stay front of mind and that you continue to build on your relationships with clients. Who knows, they might even have a legal issue they haven't gotten around to dealing with yet.

I know a lawyer who contacts ten of his clients a month just to check in. Every month he gets at least one set of new instructions. Touching base with clients can either be done the traditional way (face-to-face, phone, personalised email) or you can touch base with them via an automated email marketing platform, whichever you prefer. I would say, though, that if you aren't doing this because you're time-poor, start investing some money into automation to ensure that you're getting this done every month.

Some key ways to improve your responsiveness (and therefore your client's satisfaction) include:

1. Acknowledge your leads quickly
Whether it's online, by phone or by email (automated or not), it's important to respond to new enquiries quickly, before they go somewhere else. Clients often want a solution and they want it fast in order to reduce their anxiety, so if you can't answer them immediately, try to implement some form of automatic email that goes out to clients as soon as they make an enquiry with your firm. That email should let them know how long they should expect to wait for you to be in touch. A good standard is same-day response for new clients, perhaps even a few hours if you can.

2. Map out the process
Clients often don't know what to expect or when to expect it. So it's your job to clearly map out what's involved to give them a clear understanding of how you will both move through the process. A great way to do this is visually via an infographic. This helps reduce anxiety for your client so in turn it should reduce the amount of times your client contacts you to find out what is happening with their transaction. It should also reduce the amount of complaints you receive because lack of clarity about the process can be a huge driver of complaints.

3. Stick to your timelines

If you give a client a timeframe, it's obviously important to stick to it, but you'd be surprised how many lawyers fail to meet this standard. Ensure you give realistic timeframes to clients, ones that take into account you getting through only half of what you hope to each day. If you don't think you will meet your previously promised timeframe, touch base with your client and discuss this with them. Often timeframes can be easily negotiated.

The more responsive you can be to your clients' needs and to the changing marketplace the better your practice will do and the more clients will recommend you to people they know.

Manage expectations

If you've been practising law for a while, you'll be very familiar with how easy it can be to take on too much and feel stressed. You might feel like clients want things in unrealistic timeframes and that they simply don't care how many other clients you have.

It's true that for every client, the most important file is their file, and they often think work can be completed a lot faster than it actually can. It's not necessarily that they are too demanding; it's normally that they don't understand how long it takes for work to be completed. It follows that if you can regularly manage your clients' expectations, your work week will be a lot less frantic and your clients will be a lot happier with your service.

The first step in managing expectations is to understand exactly what the clients expect to see happen on their file and how they expect their relationship with you to work. This will require you to ask some fairly detailed questions of your clients at the outset, including what the objective is, how urgent the matter is, what result is desired, whether there are any pressing deadlines, what their communication preferences are, and whether they have any budgetary constraints. Asking these questions not only gives you an understanding of their expectations, but also allows you to see whether or not the client is unknowingly holding unrealistic expectations.

Some of the biggest complaints lawyers receive are about clients' expectations not being met. Often this is because the clients had expectations that the lawyer was not aware of, or because the lawyer failed to set realistic expectations at the outset. Once you've established some expectations with clients, it's important to walk through exactly what's likely to happen in the course of the matter and how you intend to address any potential risks or problems.

Showing the clients the different outcomes that could happen in their matter and preparing contingency plans for each will help them understand how the their matter will progress. This is particularly true for any lawyer working in litigious areas of law.

It's also important to be realistic about the risk of not meeting your clients' desired objectives. Remember not to oversell or sugarcoat the potential outcomes, as this will only lead to client disappointment. If you're setting reasonable and realistic expectations with clients who are reasonable themselves, you're likely to receive fewer frantic phone calls and fewer client complaints.

When it comes to fees, you will also need to set very clear expectations and manage them along the way. Perhaps ask if your client has a budget in mind. If you charge by the hour, try to estimate accurately how long you think the matter will take you. If you charge fixed fees, try to be really clear about the scope of services that fall within that fee. If the cost estimate or the scope of work changes, be sure to have another discussion with your client. Remember, no matter how brilliant your legal outcome, a surprise bill will most often lead to a client being dissatisfied.

Be consistent

Savvy business people understand how important it is to be consistent, not only in the way that you approach your business or your marketing campaigns, but in particular how you engage with your customers.

Clients need to have confidence in us. They need to know that we deliver on our promises every time, not just when it's convenient or when we're not very busy. If we're able to consistently deliver good service and if we consistently mean what we say and say what we mean, if we consistently under-promise and over-deliver, the potential for your law firm to not only grow but reach extraordinary heights is incredible. But more than this, it will certainly put you ahead of your competitors.

Think of some of the biggest players in the fast food industry, such as McDonald's or Starbucks. They are almost always consistent in the way they deliver their product or service. While you aren't necessarily hoping to be the next McDonald's of the legal services world, what we know is that when clients choose those brands over an unknown competitor, they're not necessarily doing so because the product is superior; they're making that choice because they know that brand has a reputation for consistency and they know what they're going to get.

Therefore, try to be consistent with your marketing campaigns. Consider the marketing messages you're sending out. Are they consistent in their tone? Are they consistent in their content? Are you delivering on your promises every time? Are you delivering the same level of service consistently for each client and throughout a transaction?

Service levels are one of the most important things to be consistent with. In fact, I remember, a few years ago, a financial adviser I know contacted me when I was on holiday in Bali. It was six am; I happened to be awake at the time so I simply dealt with the enquiry right there and then. When I was on the phone with him, he queried what time it was in Bali and I told him. He was shocked and also very impressed at how responsive I was. He shared this story with many other people. He raved about how I was on holiday and still dealt with his enquiry quickly and efficiently. That financial planner referred four clients to me over the next three months. What I had to manage was an expectation of immediate response times, but I was able to do that.

Now, I'm not saying you need to deal with every client at six am on holiday, but prompt efficient service is an overriding objective of mine. People know when they come to me that their matters will be dealt with quickly and efficiently. That is an expectation, and it is one that I aim to meet all of the time.

Under-promise, over-deliver

Clients have come to expect value for money, so they often look for service providers that go over and above their initial offering. Businesses generally know that they need to do a bit extra to attract and retain loyal clients, but what about lawyers? Do lawyers tend to offer value-added services to their customers?

We often hear law firms boasting about how they provide exceptional client service. But these days, what is exceptional client service?

Consider this scenario. A client hires you to prepare a shareholder's agreement for a new business venture. The client instructs you, you draft the shareholder's agreement exactly according to instructions and you deliver it on time and on budget. Is this exceptional service? Probably not. When the client hired you, they expected that you would draft according to their instructions, that you would draft a legally sound document and that you would provide it on time and on budget. As such you did exactly what you were hired to do. You did your job.

Delivering exceptional client service is about doing more than your job; it's about providing extra value to your clients. There will always be other law firms that will be able to provide the work as well as you can and possibly other law firms that are willing to do it cheaper than you. Exceptional client service is one way you can truly differentiate yourself.

One way to deliver extra value to your clients is to take the time to understand what other services might help them accomplish their goal, and help them source those services.

For instance, if a client hires you to draft a shareholder's agreement, they may also need accounting advice but not even know it. By listening to their needs, you might be able to refer them to an exceptional accountant. Not only will this be assisting your client, but hopefully you'll be able to make a referral to a strategic partner who will also refer to you. While the act of referring people to strategic partners is commonplace, actively listening for potential referrals while helping your client reach their goals unfortunately is not.

Another great way to deliver extra value is to be available outside of traditional office hours. This might not be something that you're naturally inclined to provide, but perhaps you might provide it one or two days a week. Often clients who do have legal matters to address (e.g. getting a will, family-law advice) want the help but can't take time off work to come to your office. Being available out of hours helps them access you more easily while simultaneously showing how client-focused you are.

There are a multitude of ways you can provide extra value to your clients. However you decide to accomplish this goal, once you start over-delivering, you should see a lot of new referrals coming your way.

Persuasive copywriting

Copywriting is the process of developing written content that you can convey through online media or print and/or print materials. The content is primarily used for advertising or marketing and is often used to promote brand awareness or persuade clients to use your services.

To be persuasive with your copywriting, you must first thoroughly understand your service and who your current target client is. If you've read the chapters earlier in this book, you'll understand exactly who that person is that you intend to target through your copywriting. After all, once you know who you're talking to, it's much easier to write your content.

Persuasive copywriting is often used to tap into the subconscious mind of your prospective clients and make them take an action to engage with you in one way or another. The most successful copywriters help prospective clients achieve their goals first before bothering them with their marketing messages.

One way to improve your copywriting and include some persuasive content is to open any marketing material content with 'yes' questions.

For instance, if you're an intellectual property lawyer, you might say, 'Would you like to protect all that you've worked hard for?' 'Do you want to protect your trademark but have no time to figure out how to do it?' Every question where your client is answering 'yes' in their head carries them forward in the process of engaging with your brand. So whenever you want to focus on persuasive or conversion-focused copy, try to open with statements that your target audience would naturally agree with.

It's also important to appeal to your clients on an emotional level. Perhaps tell them a story on your website about why you do what you do. Often there is a strong relationship between selling and storytelling, so the more you can use storytelling techniques to get people to engage with you and appeal to them on an emotional level, the more likely you are to drive their behaviour.

It's also important that any copy you create is not only engaging and persuasive, but is also clear, concise and easy to understand. As hard as it can be for lawyers (trust me, I battle this one myself!), you shouldn't use more words than necessary.

The ability to write irresistible sales copy is an incredibly important marketing skill that you can learn or perhaps ideally outsource to professionals who do this on a daily basis. Persuasive sales copy can be used throughout your marketing materials, so it can be worthwhile paying a professional to do this for you at the outset. If you've already got all of your copy done, it's still worthwhile having a professional read through it and make recommendations.

Upselling

Most people are familiar with the concept of upselling. Upselling is a particular sales strategy where you provide opportunities to your clients to purchase related services, often for the sole purpose of making a larger sale. A popular example of upselling in law is when a client or lawyer purchases a conveyance from you and they're asked whether they also need a will.

Whilst some lawyers relate upselling to McDonald's, just think for a moment about how successful McDonald's is. Most successful businesses use upselling in one form or another. Regardless of your industry or your service, upselling can be very effective at increasing profitability.

In order to upsell effectively, it's important that you know your services (or 'offerings') intimately. For example, most people who purchase a home consider it to be a life-changing event, and with each life-changing event it's important to review your estate-planning needs. So, if you sell conveyancing and you also advise in the area of estate planning, that client can easily be upsold a will.

The more you spend time thinking about your services and how they complement each other, the more you can add value and convenience to your client (while increasing your profits). You might even choose to offer the two services in a package for a set price at a cheaper rate than instructing them on the two matters separately.

Remember, you've already done the hard work by getting the client in the door. The easiest way to profit from existing clients is to upsell another service to them. There are no marketing costs associated with the upsell, so it all counts towards profit.

It's very important when you're providing upsells that you ensure that they are related to your original service. The conversion rate dramatically increases the more your upsell service is related to the original service that was purchased. Instead of trying to sell all of your services that *might* be relevant to your client, just focus on what *is* relevant at that particular time. The easiest sale is the best sale. It also means you won't come across as too pushy.

The timing of your upsell is important. Try to upsell to them before they complete their first purchase of your services. Taking the conveyancing example, don't wait until the end of the conveyance to sell them a will. They're done, they just want to relax. In their mind the transaction is over and your relationship at that point in time is complete. Always aim to upsell to your client prior to the completion of the first service they've purchased. It also helps from an administration perspective as this additional service can simply be added to the final invoice.

I know some lawyers hate the upsell concept because they don't want to be too pushy. Fair enough, I don't want you to be pushy. No one likes someone pushing services on them – it can come across as desperate. That's why your upsell has to, as a primary objective in all instances, create value for your client. You will need to come from a place of value first and foremost if you want to upsell successfully. Fixed-fee packages of services are a fantastic way to do this. Clients generally love integrated offerings because they can get everything they want with the minimum of hassle. This gives them a perceived increase in value, but also reduces your marketing cost. Best of all, the sale doesn't feel pushy.

Upselling is an incredibly valuable skill to master, because it can not only increase your profits considerably, but also increase client satisfaction.

Cross-selling

The idea of cross-selling in law firms is quite simple and commonly used in bigger practices with multiple-service offerings. Cross-selling is simply getting a client who is already using one area of your practice to use a second or third area (i.e. a family-law client uses your estate-planning service and your conveyancing service).

The difference between upselling and cross-selling can be confusing, but generally upselling is about encouraging the client to spend more money by buying a related product or extending the current product they've already got, whereas cross-selling is actually encouraging the client to spend more money by adding more products from other categories or other service areas.

For sole practitioners experienced in multiple areas of law, the difference is quite small but important to reflect on. For instance, in the previous example of a conveyance and a will, this will be considered an upsell because a will is closely related to the purchase of a conveyance. It's a natural progression because people often update their will when they purchase a property. However, if that sole practitioner also took a conveyancing client and sold their business-law services to them, it would be considered cross-selling.

Cross-selling may not be relevant to your business if you're a sole practitioner and have a niche in a particular area, but if you have a practice that has several solicitors working across several areas, it can be extraordinarily effective in increasing profits.

As with upselling, the number one reason why lawyers aren't very successful with cross-selling is that they don't want to be pushy with their clients. The assumption that you will come across as pushy is somewhat flawed. If you openly ask your client to tell you exactly what problems they're facing and you offer them services to help them resolve those problems, you're actually doing them a favour. They've been offered help; they can then choose whether they would like that help. The key here is spending the time to understand their challenges and what keeps them up at night. The more time you focus on that, the more opportunities you have to help them with a solution. Imagine, for a moment, how many of your business clients also might have a family-law matter going on in the background.

If you are working in a firm with multiple-practice areas, it can sometimes be hard to know exactly how to cross-sell. For instance, if you are a business lawyer, you probably know very little about family law, and it can be hard to sell a service where you're not the expert. That's OK, that's easily dealt with. You don't need to know the ins and outs of family law, you just need to identify the need and then organise a consultation between your client and your colleague.

One way to help you identify the other legal needs your clients may have is to talk with your colleagues about their transactions. Perhaps in a monthly meeting you could ask a person from each practice group to share one story about a case they've worked on, how it evolved and how it was resolved. This gives you valuable information that can be used in your meetings with clients.

Cross-selling also has the added benefit that you're not simply relying on individual rainmakers to bring work in. You're taking your current clients and distributing them throughout the firm so that teams of lawyers can look after your client's needs.

Sticking to your fee estimates

Whether you provide fixed-fee quotes or fee estimates, you'd agree that the process of scoping out work to be completed and agreeing on the fees to be charged is often challenging. It is also somewhat confronting, particularly if you offer fixed-fee services, because you don't want to under-quote on the matter.

Whether you are charging fixed fees or estimates, scoping out a matter correctly is extremely important. If you fail to do this correctly, you could encounter a host of issues. Of course you can always re-scope the matter if you've missed important elements, but you run the risk of upsetting your client when you come back and ask for more money. Or if you're very busy and forget to re-scope the matter and agree on a new fee, you run the risk of losing a lot of money. Scoping a matter incorrectly also means you underestimate how much time you need to complete the matter. This can obviously affect your stress levels and can mean you're too busy to give the proper level of service expected of you.

I can't tell you how many clients have come to Legally Yours after they have seen other lawyers they have been extremely unhappy with. The number one complaint is that their lawyer estimated a certain fee and then exceeded that estimate by a long shot. Often estimated fees have doubled, leaving the client furious and fed up with the legal profession. It's understandable. If I went to buy a pair of shoes and the salesperson said they were $100, then I bought them and started wearing them only to receive another $100 invoice in the mail, I'd be annoyed too!

As with any other profession, we have the ability to spend the time scoping out work in detail so that we can provide a clear and accurate estimate of fees to clients (or, ideally, a fixed fee). If the scope changes, communicate this immediately to your client and discuss a new estimate. It's reasonable to change an estimate when the scope of work has increased. But, barring large changes to the scope of the work or unusually high levels of communication on a matter, fee estimates should be adhered to. If you're not scoping correctly, you're potentially misleading your clients.

Generally, one of the most anxiety-provoking things for a client about engaging a lawyer is the cost, regardless of who that client is. One way to stand out from the crowd is to provide fixed fees for your clients or, alternatively, a promise to stick to your fee estimates. If you do offer this service (which, frankly, all lawyers should be offering), why not advertise it on your website? It's certainly a selling point.

Don't avoid giving bad news to clients

Every lawyer, at some point or another, is required to deliver bad news to his or her client. By bad news here I'm not necessarily talking about the outcome of their matter, I'm talking about bad news that relates to something you may have done (i.e. a missed timeline or a mistake you've made). Regardless of who the client is or which area of law you specialise in, the way you deliver that bad news and manage that process will either improve or worsen your relationship with the client, so it's crucial to develop skills to deliver bad news well. Moreover, it's very important to break that bad news as soon as possible, rather than delay the giving of the news.

Obviously you need to use your judgment about when and how you deliver the bad news. Communication skills are vital to maintaining relationships with clients when delivering bad news. For example, if you are unable to complete a matter by the promised completion date, you would not want to email a client, which I know we're all tempted to do. It's important to pick up the phone and actually have a conversation with the client. This shows that you're a confident and competent lawyer who's able to handle problems with integrity.

When delivering bad news, try not to talk too much and maintain good listening skills. If you deliver bad news and spend time listening to your client, it will help your client feel understood and therefore less annoyed.

Try to identify the feelings that underlie what the person is saying and address those feelings. Don't worry about controlling the conversation or trying to fix the problem too quickly. It's okay to be uncomfortable and to listen to how your client feels, and in some instances this can in itself resolve any issue the client may have with the fact that you have bad news to deliver to them.

Certainly, learning to deliver bad news effectively can mean that an uncomfortable situation can turn into a situation that actually improves your relationship with the client and boosts your credibility. Perhaps put yourself in the client's shoes and understand the effect that it might have on the client. Be very honest and direct with your approach during the conversation and try not to beat around the bush.

The client isn't looking for you to give a long-winded explanation, they're looking to see if you can potentially provide a viable solution to the problem. Ideally, before you bring a problem to your client, see if you can come up with a solution that can reduce their concerns about a problem. For instance, if you're unable to meet a timeline, perhaps connect the client with a colleague of yours within the law firm that will be able to also work on the project to bring it to completion in a quick manner.

Ask for feedback

We all want feedback (well, I hope so!) but most of us don't ask our clients about their opinion of our service. This is particularly true if we think they haven't had a great experience with us. But how else are you to know how to improve your service and your overall customer experience?

The only way that you can guarantee a service that clients actually want to buy is to obtain client feedback and respond to that feedback by adapting your service to meet client needs. Some of the most innovative companies in the world are fantastic at doing this. They effectively design their services and products, bit by bit, based on what their clients are saying about their products. Think of Apple. They often pivot their services based on real-time feedback from clients. This provides them with strong competitive advantages in the marketplace.

Apart from being able to improve your service, it also helps you to understand whether you're meeting or surpassing client expectations. If you're not meeting expectations, it's better to know about it so you can make changes so you don't start losing clients. If you are meeting or exceeding expectations in some areas, you know what to keep doing.

If you regularly send out customer feedback surveys, all of this information can be collected and reviewed monthly. There are free online resources such as SurveyMonkey where you can create a link to a survey and include that link in your final invoices or in your emails so you can collect data in an automated way.

In addition to the normal feedback questions, your survey may also include a question about how your client found you and what other services they may need from you. This helps guide your business and marketing decisions. For example, if you have a number of clients who found you through Facebook, you know to put more time or money into Facebook as it's an effective marketing channel. Or perhaps you have clients who are currently instructing you on a conveyance but they also need some estate-planning advice. If you don't currently offer that advice, maybe it's time to, because the demand is there. These additional measurable bits of data help you change and adapt your practice as needed.

Feedback from your clients can also be beneficial to identify who your business ambassadors are. These are people that give you very high scores or rave about your business. These are the clients who are important to contact regularly and build strong and mutual business relationships with. They are also the clients you should be asking for testimonials or referrals. More often than not, these clients are so happy with your service that they want to help you.

Asking for feedback can be a little scary at times. Some lawyers just don't want to know. I'd encourage you to think of feedback as valuable (and free) insights into your business. It's effectively business advice that helps you create a service that people rave about. Doesn't everyone want that?

Ask clients for referrals

Lawyers are very comfortable with referrals and are often very good at developing partnerships with other businesses in order to give and receive referrals. But what many lawyers don't do is actually ask their clients directly for referrals. They assume that if they do a job well that business will simply come to them through referrals.

However, clients that use your service aren't necessarily very focused on helping you grow your practice or getting more clients for you, so it may not even enter their minds. It might be as simple as saying to a client that you're really pleased that they enjoyed working with you and you'd really appreciate it if they could pass your name along to anyone else that they know that might be interested in your services. You could even leave some extra business cards with them, making it very easy for them to pass on your business card onto someone else.

Alternatively, you may forward something in the mail that allows people to send you the name of a friend or family member who might be interested in your services. You might even offer an incentive by way of a gift voucher for that referral.

Try not to let your own fears get in the way of building your practice. Referrals will certainly increase your client base, and the more referrals you ask for, the more referrals you will get.

The best way that you can increase your referral campaigns is to teach your customers how to refer to you. You may want to provide a cheat sheet with your core value proposition and a few testimonials. That might be in the form of a brochure that talks about what you do and why someone should choose you.

Whichever area of law you work in, referrals can certainly be the lifeblood of your business.

Reward referral sources

While rewards (monetary or otherwise) are helpful, they are not essential to drive referrals. Certainly, you may have some strategic partners or clients who are very happy to refer to you and don't expect anything in return – and, of course, the primary reason that anyone should refer to you is because you provide an exceptional service – but most people in one way or another do like to be rewarded for their referral. I'm not necessarily talking about monetary rewards here. Rewards can take the form of recognition. Recognising individuals who make successful referrals to your business can be incredibly powerful.

For instance, you may wish to send a personalised note, or you may wish to call and thank them or perhaps send a little gift. You may even wish to put on a once-a-year luncheon with people who have made successful referrals to your practice.

If you're going to offer rewards to clients or referral partners, try experimenting with different types of rewards and see what resonates with people. Perhaps start with a low-cost reward such as a personalised note. Don't let the time this takes put you off, either. Remember, you saved time and money on marketing by receiving that referral. You may even choose to see what your competitors are doing in this space and go one step further.

Whatever your approach, providing recognition for the referral is the most important thing you can do to keep getting more referrals, so make sure when people are supporting your practice that you're recognising their efforts.

Chapter 6
Planning For Your Future

"Someone's sitting in the shade today because someone planted a tree a long time ago."
Warren Buffet

Planning is a critical part of any business. Without planning, you don't know where you're going or how you're going to get there. It's like driving to an unknown destination without a map. You can easily go off course. This can inevitably lead to a lot of wasted time and money and, particularly if you're just starting out, you can't be wasting either.

If you run a small practice, it can be very tempting to neglect planning completely, particularly if you feel like it is a time-consuming or overwhelming process that takes you away from revenue-generating activities.

But it doesn't have to be time-consuming or overwhelming. Some of the best business plans I've seen can actually fit on a page, and some of the best planning exercises take minutes, not days, to complete. Let's have a look at some of them.

How much business do you actually need?

Whether you're starting a law firm or planning for the future, it is always important to ask yourself how many clients you actually need. So many lawyers start out in business simply by trying to obtain as many clients as possible. Often they think that the first goal is to use up all of their own personal capacity, and grow the firm by hiring more staff to accommodate their growing client base. They work harder, faster and later in order to increase profitability. But you know what these lawyers all have in common? They're often burnt out and dissatisfied with their lives. They feel out of control, as if their practice is controlling their lifestyle. In addition, they often feel concerned that the quality of their advice is suffering because of the time pressure they are under. Sound familiar?

It's understandable. This is how it's always been. But what if you knew where you were going? What if you had a plan? I'm not talking about a detailed fifty-page business plan. That's somewhat archaic these days. I'm talking about a simple revenue-based plan.

I'd encourage you to think about the life you want to live. This includes:

- how much money you want to make
- how much time with your family you want to spend
- how much annual leave you want to take
- how stressed or relaxed you want to be.

Let's start with the revenue goal. What target would you like to reach this year? Let's say it's $200,000 and you charge clients by the hour. You have fifty-two weeks in the year, so let's say you want to work forty-eight of them and take four weeks of leave a year. That means you need to make approximately $4166 plus change a week. In one week, let's say you spend 80% of your time on billable work, and let's say you work 9 am – 6 pm with an hour for lunch. That means you have thirty-two hours of billable work you can complete. So you need to ensure that you charge at least $130 an hour. Now most lawyers charge at least twice that hourly rate, so even if you have very few clients and only complete twenty of your hours a week, you will be hitting your target.

So if we know that hitting even half of your possible billable hours a week will hit your target, how many clients do you need per month to hit those billable hours? If each of your matters take about ten hours you know you need at least thirteen new matters a month.

When you start to plan backwards, you start to get very clear about exactly how many new clients per month you need to reach your revenue goals. For most people, thirteen new clients a month sounds like a lot of work and a lot of marketing spend. Knowing what your targets are helps you plan for the future. Not only can you reflect on your hourly rate (perhaps it needs to increase) but you can also reflect on how you will market your services more effectively and efficiently. By planning in this way from the outset, you don't get stuck working at rates that don't serve your goals, and you don't get sidetracked with marketing efforts that won't bring in the volume of clients you need.

If you're tentative about increasing your hourly rate, perhaps you need to be considering how much value you're giving to each of your clients. If you're giving your clients a lot of value (and demonstrating that value well), you never feel like your hourly rate is too high, and your clients won't, either.

If your clients aren't responding well to your price point and you feel you are demonstrating and providing large amounts of value, look at the kind of clients you're attracting. Are they the clients you want or do you need to reflect on whether your target market is right for you? Fundamentally, when you do your numbers, it might become apparent that you're targeting the wrong clients, the clients that drag their feet and don't want to pay. If so, you'll need to revisit your 'ideal client' and your marketing to see where you might be going wrong.

Another thing you could consider is implementing a different billing model. How would your targets change if you moved to a retainer model or a fixed-fee model? How would your lifestyle change if you were working with clients who had you on a $4,000 retainer per month, every month? How many clients would you need then?

Knowing what you're aiming towards helps you to reflect on the methods you will use to get there. Why not test out a few different methods and see what works best for yourself and for your clients?

Goal setting

Most lawyers understand the importance of goal setting but rarely make time to create goals. Goal setting in its essence is the process of deciding exactly what you want to accomplish in life and in business (and health and love) and creating a plan to achieve that result. It's more than just having an idea about what you want to achieve, it's also about breaking down the goals and creating a plan to implement consistent action so as to achieve those goals. After all, goals without action are just words.

Goals are important because they enable you to have a clear direction for your business and they guide you in your decision-making processes. For instance, you may establish a goal of increasing your sales by 20% in the next financial year. You may then realise from that goal that you need additional training in sales and marketing to reach that goal, or that you need to hire someone to help you. Without that goal, you may not realise that you need a hand to get to the next stage in your practice.

What I see most often with lawyers is that they often haven't started their year off with a set of goals but they have one long 'to-do' list with a hundred items on it. The items aren't categorised, and no time is spent reflecting on whether these items will actually generate the outcomes they are after.

So, instead of having a never-ending 'to-do' list, why not simply write goals in the four main areas of your life: health, wealth and love and relationships? They don't have to be extensive, but they do have to be goals that you feel are out of reach. Otherwise, they're not really goals, right? By having goals, you gain perspective on what you want to achieve in all areas of your life, not just work. Once you have decided on your big goals, start breaking them down into actionable and manageable SMART goals.

Most people will have heard of the SMART acronym when setting goals. SMART stands for specific, measurable, attainable, relevant and time-bound. These are incredibly important when it comes to your goals.

Specific means that goals should be clearly defined so it's clear exactly what action you need to take. It effectively demonstrates the what, why and how. For instance, you may wish to better manage your client contacts so that you can start an email marketing campaign. In this example, the 'what' would be to implement a client management system to record and manage your client details. The 'how' might be using a cloud-based CRM product, such as Zoho or MailChimp, and the 'why' might be so you can send monthly updates to all of your clients and help raise your profile.

The M stands for measurable and basically means that every goal you set should be measurable so that you can tangibly review whether or not you've accomplished the goal. For instance, you may wish to set a date upon which you wish to achieve the goal previously mentioned. The metric then is whether the CRM is operational by the particular date you set.

A stands for achievable. Effectively, goals should be challenging and out of your reach (when you set them), but achievable. Ideally, you must possess the appropriate knowledge, skills and abilities needed to achieve the goal or have third-party resources that you can use in order to attain that goal. After all, you don't want to set a goal to be a doctor if you've never studied medicine! Achievable goals help to motivate you, whereas impossible goals can demotivate you.

R stands for results. The focus here is on being very clear and specific about what you want to achieve. It helps you determine whether you've reached your goal. So the specific result you may wish to achieve by implementing your email marketing campaign is an increase in new instructions from your current client base by 5%.

Ideally all goals should be time-bound so that they're linked to a particular time frame that creates a sense of urgency for you. A great practice to get into is to start writing SMART goals every quarter and then break those goals down into monthly or weekly actions in order to achieve those goals.

Create revenue targets

Speaking of creating goals, it is critical that you set SMART goals for revenue targets. All too often, many law firms fail to set revenue targets. This is particularly true for sole practitioners who often simply review the previous year's revenue and add on what they would like to see as a reasonable growth rate. Setting a revenue target in this way isn't very strategic. It often means that the practitioner simply tries to work harder and harder to reach the goal, often resulting in burn-out.

Before you implement a SMART goal in relation to your revenue, try working backwards (as outlined above). Start by looking at what you want overall in terms of how hard you work, how much you want to work and what kind of clients you want to work with.

Understanding your current revenue data will also help you. Try to review your average transaction value, how many matters you worked on and how many clients you served. Did you upsell or cross-sell your services? Did you have a lot of repeat clients? How were your conversion and retention rates? By reviewing this data, you will get clearer about what might be an achievable revenue target for the following year.

It might be, for example, that you're receiving an appropriate number of enquiries, but that your conversion rate is quite low. That helps you understand that your marketing campaigns are working adequately, but that perhaps you need some more sales training. If you get some sales training, you could assume that your conversion rates will increase and your revenue target can be set a bit higher.

Alternatively, maybe the quality of enquiries isn't right for your particular area of business, so your marketing channels need to be reviewed. Understanding these processes and knowing exactly where things are going wrong can dramatically improve revenue without too much additional work. For instance, if you are aware of your conversion rate in your law firm and focus on improving it, you may be able to double the amount of clients you convert and hence have a higher revenue target.

The more you understand, the more you can take measurable action towards increasing your revenue goals.

Obviously increasing revenue is important, but you also need to understand that increase within the confines of your profit and loss statement. Otherwise you may increase revenue but decrease profit. Ideally, you need to be increasing your revenue at a greater rate than your operational expenses, so that you can achieve greater profit.

Your profit and loss statement will also give you an understanding as to seasonal fluctuations in your practice, which will help you plan when you may like to take a holiday. If you're not quite sure exactly where to start, ask yourself the following questions:

- In the next twelve months, how many new clients would you like?
- What will your average transaction value be?
- How many of those clients will be repeat clients in the next twelve months?
- What is your average conversion rate?
- What are your operating expenses?
- In particular, what are your marketing expenses and where can your marketing dollar have the biggest effect?

These are the big picture questions that help you understand exactly where you are, where you'd like to go and how you can get there.

Continue to ask questions

Over the past couple of decades, the global economic climate has changed significantly. In a changing climate, you need to be able to respond and adapt appropriately so you can continue to thrive even during downtimes.

Continuing to ask yourself questions in business helps you understand your current situation and helps you identify ways in which you can innovate and pivot your business model to address a change in environment. Continue to ask yourself questions, but also to continue to ask your client base questions about what they want and need.

Think of the example of Kodak. They continued along with the idea that their customers wanted physical photos and would not move to the digital age. But what Kodak failed to realise was that they weren't in the business of photos, they were in the business of creating memories, and people wanted those memories to be created and accessible instantly. Had they asked themselves and their customers how they would best be able to help their clients capture and share their Kodak moments, then perhaps things may have gone differently for them.

It highlights the importance of asking yourself what business you're actually in. As a lawyer, are you in the business of providing legal advice? Probably yes, but on a deeper level you're in the business of reducing anxiety and solving people's problems. Just as book publishers aren't necessarily in the book business, they're in the business of storytelling. Once you get clear about exactly what you are providing for your clients, you can start to figure out ways to remain relevant as you move into the future.

Kodak, like many lawyers these days, didn't truly believe that there would be a new way of delivering moments to their clients. They didn't believe that digital would be so disruptive. They made the mistake of assuming that their business model would stay relevant. What we know in the legal profession is that the model is starting to change, and the current model at some point or another is going to end, so it's crucial to consider what business we're in and what our clients ultimately want.

Consistent action

Leonardo da Vinci once said, 'It had long since come to my attention that people of accomplishment rarely sat back and let things happen to them. They went out and happened to things'.

One of the biggest and most important things that you can do in your business life is to continue to take action over a long period of time. After all, it's not only what we do in our practice that helps shape a practice, but it's what we do consistently. It's incredible how many lawyers have great ideas, but actually never take action. Then, in a year or two, they complain that they haven't received what they want.

Sometimes where lawyers get stuck is that they don't do anything unless they can complete it perfectly. This fear of failure means they don't start anything that doesn't seem completely achievable. I know, as lawyers, we're told we can never make a mistake, so it's hard to get out of that mindset, but if you get hung up on perfection you won't take action. So, get hung up on taking action! Get perfect at consistency, but let perfection go. I routinely do things that seem impossible and scare me half to death. Each year, because of this, I grow as a person and as a business owner.

Take baby steps; every step forward is better than doing nothing. Ten baby steps taken over time can help you to reach the overall goal that might allow you to fulfil your dreams. Those that are incredibly successful do things consistently every single day, because they understand that creating the practice of their dreams is about the single step. The challenge, of course, is getting the self-discipline to take consistent steps every single day.

Here are some tips that might help:

- Use rituals. This is one of the most important tips when it comes to consistent action. Having a routine set up in the morning can often not only help you achieve your goals, but also set the context for the rest of your day. Perhaps there's one action that you can take every day to work towards a goal that you wish to achieve.

- Focus on and be responsible for the actions, not the results. Think about someone for example who needs to lose forty kilos. It can feel like an overwhelming goal, so if you're not losing weight every single day you might give up. Instead, if you take responsibility for and simply focus on showing up at the gym every single day, the results start to speak for themselves because they come from consistent action. It allows you to focus on the here and now and not the future, which allows you to be a lot more relaxed during the process.

- Make sure to keep your goals in plain sight to remind
  you of what you're looking to achieve. Have them
  around you, look at them every day, have them on your
  screensaver, write them on your whiteboard. Enjoy the
  process of creating a life that you'll love and try not to
  get distracted about everything else around you. Break
  that goal up into little pieces and then focus on getting
  one thing done every single day.

After all, you know exactly what you need to do to create the life
that you love, so it's time to start doing it.

Take time out to be creative

Often as lawyers, we're overwhelmed with all that there is to do.
It seems there's no time to take lunch, let alone take time out to
reflect on your practice. But when you schedule your day from
start to finish and have no time to step back, it can actually get
in the way of creating better and stronger results. Apart from the
obvious benefits of taking some time out (i.e. reducing stress and
'overwhelm'), taking some time out actually helps you find creative
solutions to some of the problems you may be facing.

While we all feel a sense of urgent responsibility for the work we
do on a day-to-day basis, and we justify that we don't have the time
to be able to take time for ourselves, taking time out is actually part
of your professional responsibility. After all, no one likes working
with a tired, overworked lawyer. When you're constantly draining
all of your cognitive resources, there's no way that you can be as
productive as you could possibly be, so your performance is likely
to decline.

We don't have an unlimited amount of energy; it's important
to take rests to preserve your sanity, de-stress and improve the
quality of your life. The more time out you take to get back in
touch with your ideas (and your inspiration), the more you achieve
creative insights. It's these insights that help you to continue

to be innovative, with new ideas about how to do things better, more quickly and more efficiently in your practice. It's like those moments early in the morning when we randomly have a brilliant idea. Those ideas come because we have created the space for them to come.

Regardless of how busy you feel in your everyday life, remember that the benefits of taking time out are not only to decrease stress and increase creativity, but also help to increase productivity. Adding something as simple as a ten-minute meditation at the start of your day, or a walk through the park at lunchtime can help reduce your stress, re-energise you, increase your productivity and help you engage more meaningfully with your business and clients.

Income-generating activities

For lawyers to be successful, they must master their time and focus on the right activities. The right activities obviously need to be income-generating activities, so that you're focusing the majority of your time on activities that will generate revenue (and ideally profit) for your practice.

Of course, spending time working with your current clients will bring you revenue, but what do you do to ensure future revenue? Luckily, there are some really simple and quick income-generating activities that every law firm owner should focus on every single day.

The first is to be really clear about what your clients are looking for and what their particular challenges are. This requires that you create an environment in which your prospective or current clients feel comfortable to openly share their thoughts and feel like you'll listen. If you offer consultations, try making them free. Use that time to ask your prospective clients exactly what their challenges are and what they need from you. I know a free consultation may sound counter-intuitive given the subject heading, but this information is incredibly valuable as it helps you understand how to sell your services to your prospective clients. The more you know, the easier it is to sell. The more you sell your services, the more income you generate.

Feel free, of course, to limit your free consultations. Perhaps create five half-hour slots in your week where you offer 'strategy sessions' or 'discovery sessions' to your clients to discuss their goals and what they need. They might start with having a simple legal question about how to create the best structure for their business, for example, which gives you an opportunity to share your knowledge and expertise and help them understand how they might get there using your services. It's important when you do this that you're not trying to aggressively sell your services, but that you're trying to give them something of value.

One of the easiest ways to grow your practice is to start regularly looking for speaking opportunities. Some are paid, and some unpaid, but all will be beneficial to your practice. This is more than waiting for speaking opportunities to come to you; instead, start finding out which organisations your target market belongs to and then contact those organisations to see if they would be interested in hearing something of value from you. By showing your knowledge in a 'one-to-many' rather than 'one-to-one' capacity, you not only raise your profile but you also position yourself as the expert, and clients want to work with experts.

Ideally, networking offline and face-to-face with your ideal client can be incredibly valuable, because you can clearly understand who your ideal client is, what their challenges are and what they're looking for in a lawyer. But this can also be a huge time waster if you're not careful. Carefully select the networking events that you attend so that you're not just going to random events in the vague hope of meeting a new client.

I'd recommend setting two income-generating activities to complete every day. They might be as simple as emailing a prospective client, having a lunch meeting, going to a networking event or sending out a speaking proposal. Whatever it is, try to be consistent in those actions so you're focusing on things that propel you towards higher revenue and higher profit in your practice.

Incentivise your team

In a challenging economic environment, you need to be able to get the most out of your team. To get the best productivity from your team, you will need to be able to incentivise them and keep them happy in their roles. After all, it's more cost-effective to retain and improve existing staff than to find new staff.

Incentivising lawyers is traditionally done through pay rises and large bonuses, but this can be difficult when the economic climate is tough. So let's consider some other more creative solutions to incentivise your team.

Even if you do have money to spare, it's worth considering whether money is actually the right motivational tool for your team. Perhaps the focus needs to be on creating an employee-friendly practice that aims to boost morale and increase productivity through motivation. For instance, you may wish to offer an additional annual leave day for each staff member on his or her birthday. This is something that costs little but which staff members often rave about to others.

If time is more valuable to your staff members than money, you may decide to allow staff members to buy additional holidays and work less. Alternatively, you may allow your employees to have a more flexible schedule. For instance they may prefer to work outside the traditional nine-to-five (or eight-to-seven!) office hours.

As long as it suits your practice and your client base, it can be a great incentive for attracting and keeping higher-performing employees. After all, flexibility is somewhat rare when it comes to working in law.

If you're a bit unsure about how this might work but would like to try it out, you may wish to select a number of employees based on eligibility or type of role. Before you implement it, discuss with them what their needs are. For instance, they may prefer starting work an hour earlier and leaving an hour earlier, or maybe they would prefer working a longer day one day during the week and a shorter day another.

You may also wish to offer employees corporate memberships to local gyms or sporting clubs. Club memberships not only help promote employee wellbeing, but can often be used for a variety of business networking events.

One of the easiest and most cost-effective ways to incentivise your lawyers is to show appreciation often, not only directly to them but also to their families. Perhaps you could have an annual family day or family evening where your staff can bring their family into work. Apart from getting to know your staff better, you'll also be creating a collegiate environment.

Do the work you love to do

Sometimes at work it can feel like the 'to-do' list is never ending. No matter how many hours you put in, it's difficult to see an end in sight. It can make you feel unmotivated and can certainly make you procrastinate. Have you noticed, though, that other times you can work for hours on end and actually feel energised when you've completed some work? What's the difference? Why, when we're focused on one thing, it can elicit a negative reaction and when we focus on another, we get a positive response?

The reality is that most people don't mind actually working hard when they're excited about what they're accomplishing. When they're doing things they really like to do, it starts feeling easy. Try looking at your workload and the things that you do, day in, day out, and understand the difference between the work you love to do (or at least don't mind getting up in the morning for) and the work that you can't stand doing.

Then focus on generating more of the work that you enjoy doing and minimise the amount of time on tasks that you can't stand to do or that drain you of energy. It sounds like a very simple task, but for most lawyers it's simply about reflecting on what we do. By paying a bit of attention to the type of work that you love and the type of work that drains you, you can start to enjoy your work a hell of a lot more.

The things that we enjoy in work are generally things that we're naturally good at. If we're good at a particular skill, we often find ourselves honing our abilities in this area and skilling ourselves up. Once you become good at a particular area of work and enjoy it, often people value what you do and then money ultimately follows (I'm assuming here what you love to do is also something that brings you some money!). It's important to find the work that you really enjoy doing and that you're passionate about. Start to create a balance in your work life where you're doing more of the work you want to do instead of the work you have to do.

If you're not entirely sure what it is that you love to do in your current role, it's worthwhile investing some time thinking about that question. What do you find yourself talking about? What are your strengths? What are your talents? What are things that come naturally to you?

Start to explore new things, new types of law perhaps, new elements of your practice. Do some reading, learn about new things and try them out. Remember fear and the limitations in their minds are what stops people from finding a new element in their role that they really enjoy.

Now, delegate or stop doing the rest.

Build elements of automation and scalability into your business

If you're like most sole practitioners, you've started out as a one-person show. Maybe you had a client or two, maybe not. You have your laptop, your skills and your vision. Your goal is to grow, to increase revenue while decreasing operational costs, and therefore to increase profits.

The problem is that the day-to-day running of what is effectively a small business can be incredibly overwhelming. If you work on hourly rates and you get a few clients in the door, it can be hard to take a step back. You want to just keep working those hours and driving money into your practice. You not only do all of the legal work but all of the accounting work, answering the phone calls, returning emails, all of the marketing, ordering stationery, etc. But doesn't this limit you? Of course it does. If you work in this way, you're always going to be limited by the fact that your time is limited. You only ever have twenty-four hours in a day.

Building some form of scalability in your business allows you to expand your business and increase revenue while keeping operational expenditure steady. Even if you're not ready to grow at that rate or looking at scalability at the moment, there are certain things that you can implement into your business today that can set you up for growth in the future.

First, have a look back over the tips in this book that talk about systemising and automation. These will help you to free up your time and allow operational costs to remain low.

Other systems that can be very helpful are client-relationship management tools and cloud-based accounting software. They help to streamline processes so that they can be managed either automatically or by other people working virtually. The more processes and systems you put in place, the more you can remove yourself from the everyday running of your practice.

Ultimately, this means you can spend more time on things that generate more revenue. You might choose to spend this time working on client matters, or otherwise building a practice that can be sold. While it seems like you're the core of your practice, you don't want to be. Ideally, you want as many elements of your practice as possible to run without you. For a practice to be saleable, you need to be able remove yourself from it.

As this sounds entirely unfeasible to many lawyers, most remain unable to sell their practices at the end of the day. Of course, not every law firm is designed for scalability and not every business model is easy to change. However, making a few key adjustments in what you do can make the difference for your firm.

By trimming the fat in your business processes, automating as many of your routine processes as possible and decreasing the cost of providing those services, your business model can scale a lot more effectively. You may also wish to reduce operational costs by becoming a virtual law firm. This, in itself, can cut out a lot of high overheads. Or perhaps you could start hiring staff on a flexible basis to support you as and when needed, rather than having full-time employees.

It is also my fundamental belief that law firms need to start thinking about their services as product offerings. Each service can be a product for a specific fee, and each service has a detailed outline of what is included and has its own value proposition. Once your services are products, other people can sell those services on your behalf. This enables you to hire salespeople to drive sales to you rather than having to skill up on how to drive sales yourself.

Some firms are already doing this in the areas of estate planning and conveyancing. I believe that eventually market forces will push practically all law firms towards turning at least some of their services into products in the future.

Educate yourself in business

Many of the bigger law firms offer extensive in-house development programs, covering various areas of legal skills, knowledge and practice management. Some of them also cover some basic business skills. But if you're not in these firms and you want to start your own practice, you often have limited knowledge in the areas of management, finance and marketing.

I find this very interesting when I look at some of the legal innovators in Australia. The majority of them are lawyers who have worked in transactional areas of law, often relating to business or finance. They seem to have a lot of business and finance knowledge as well as legal knowledge, making it easier for them to transition into the business world.

But for most lawyers making the leap into sole practice, the lack of knowledge in these areas can feel overwhelming. Starting a new practice is a big undertaking, and much bigger than most realise. Many businesses fail within the first couple of years and there are many pitfalls in the journey that could completely destroy your dream.

There's an easy fix to this – spend time educating yourself in these areas. I know, sounds obvious, right? But how many business books have you read this year? By continuing to educate yourself in these areas, you will keep your creativity alive and you will start accumulating knowledge that can help you move forward when other firms stay stagnant.

It's important to read business books, but it's more important to read the right books. One of the best books that I can recommend for every lawyer looking to start their own practice without wasting a lot of money is *The Lean Startup* by Eric Ries. The insights in this book are priceless and can be applied to almost any business. There are some incredible entrepreneurial books related to business and management these days that can help you create a practice that is quite innovative (and, hence, you'll have a point of difference from the outset).

Marketing books can also be incredibly useful, including *Guerrilla Marketing* by Jay Conrad Levinson. It's very useful because it's geared to marketing on a shoestring budget and helps you to appear big when you're actually just quite a small firm or perhaps a sole practitioner.

Try spending some time online or in your local bookstore reviewing the array of business books available. Pick some books that inspire you and then commit to reading one book at least every month (which is less than half an hour a few times a week). Within six months, you'll be filled with new insights, inspiration and knowledge to be able to process what's happening for your practice and adapt it for the future.

Hire people with the same vision

If you're looking at hiring staff for your firm, you'll probably be looking at their skill set, whether they're the right cultural fit and whether they have a strong work ethic. Yes, these things are important, but fundamentally it will be crucial to also find someone who shares your firm's vision for the future. If you have other people who are working with the same vision, you're halfway there. They will be ambassadors for what you want to achieve, and the way in which they work will support your goals.

So before you bring a new person on board, make sure that you clearly explain your vision for the future of your firm. Be clear with them about your objectives and your strategies for achieving your vision and see what they say. Are they getting excited?

One way to attract great people to your firm is to start sharing your 'why' with the world. In this way you will start attracting people that share the same 'why'.

I remember posting an ad for a business development manager for Legally Yours. I talked little about the duties and a lot about the vision of the company and what I wanted to create. I talked about who I was and the type of person I wanted to work with. I talked about what we could achieve together and why we should strive to achieve it. The person who got the job (and is now my business partner) is someone who said at her interview, 'I felt like you were speaking directly to me'. She now shares our vision every day, and we never seem to disagree about the way forward.

The more you start to share the story of why you're doing what you're doing, the more people will want to join you on your journey. These are the people that will stick by you through the highs and the lows, because they share your broader vision. These are the people you want.

Do what scares you

One of the most damaging things you can do to your career is to continue to do what you're comfortable doing. We all know that, to some extent, putting yourself outside of your comfort zone is crucial to career success, yet few of us do it.

Probably because we feel terrified. As lawyers we're risk-averse and it's easy to stop yourself from doing things that are scary. Things that are outside your comfort zone can paralyse you and you can reason with yourself about why you shouldn't do what you know you need to do. It's important in those moments to stop thinking and start focusing on doing one step at a time.

Facing a fear helps us feel alive and helps to inspire you. It's incredibly motivating when you prove to yourself that you can do it. It doesn't have to be overwhelming. You don't have to address all of your fears immediately. But the people who do this successfully are able to make an incredibly positive impact and create new opportunities to drive their practice forward at an accelerated pace. If you want to differentiate yourself from the competition, you have to be willing to try new things.

Generally, your comfort zone relates to things that keep your anxiety at bay. They're activities that you're used to doing that won't make you feel anxious and uneasy. So conversely, things that are outside your comfort zone can raise your anxiety levels. But surprisingly, small amounts of anxiety can be incredibly beneficial.

The right level of anxiety is that which pushes us to perform productively, not which leads you into a panic zone. Panic creates procrastination. You need the sweet spot, the one where the anxiety is definitely there but you're not so overwhelmed that you do nothing. In this zone, you can continue to grow and accomplish a great deal. Each time you go into that zone, the zone changes. Suddenly the things that seemed scary now seem manageable, and the things that previously made you panic seem anxiety-provoking but not overwhelming. This is growth.

So try to get out of your comfort zone often. This in itself will increase your comfort zone over time. If, for instance, you're scared of public speaking, you can push yourself outside of your comfort zone by speaking to a small crowd and, slowly over time, increase the size of that audience.

How far you want to push yourself out of your comfort zone is dependent on the level of anxiety you're comfortable with, but the trick is to consistently push yourself further and further so that you continue to learn and grow.

Over time you will get more comfortable with the fact that the worst thing you can do is fail, but even a failed attempt at something is a success because you had the courage to take a risk.

Writing this book is the scariest thing I've ever done in my business life, but I'm glad I've done it. Hopefully along the way I've helped some of you in your journey. To your success!

By the way, I've always wanted to write this …

The End!

Afterword

What I've given you in this book are some simple and easy-to-apply marketing strategies, tips and tools that every successful law firm I know uses to stand out from the crowd, attract more clients and make more money.

Whether you apply one tip a week or ten, taking action is vital. I encourage you to get out of your comfort zone and start challenging yourself to do the things that scare you. Whether that's digital marketing, speaking events or sales funnels, don't let your own fear or the traditional 'lawyer' model limit you. You can do whatever you want to do, and you can have a lot of fun doing it. Create the firm you want and the life you want, one step at a time. Here's to those steps turning into a run!

Author Biography

Mira **Stammers** is a lawyer, entrepreneur, academic, consultant, author and public speaker. Her mission is simple: to teach lawyers how to create and execute effective marketing strategies to increase their profitability.

A pioneer in legal innovation, Mira is most commonly known for being the co-founder of legallyyours.com.au, one of the first legal marketplaces in the world. She writes regularly for legal and business publications, and provides realistic and powerful marketing advice to lawyers and law firms (see mirastammers.com.au for consulting and speaking event bookings).

www.ingramcontent.com/pod-product-compliance
Lightning Source LLC
Chambersburg PA
CBHW021939190326
41519CB00009B/1066